William Thomson

On Renascence Drama

Or, history made visible

William Thomson

On Renascence Drama
Or, history made visible

ISBN/EAN: 9783337394158

Printed in Europe, USA, Canada, Australia, Japan

Cover: Foto ©ninafisch / pixelio.de

More available books at **www.hansebooks.com**

ON

RENASCENCE DRAMA

OR

HISTORY MADE VISIBLE

BY

WILLIAM THOMSON, F.R.C.S., F.L.S.

"Fame and foundation of the English weal."

"And in the midst
Thou stand'st as if some mystery thou didst!"

BEN JONSON.

MELBOURNE:

SANDS & McDOUGALL, COLLINS STREET WEST.

1880.

CONTENTS.

CHAPTER   PAGE

I. HOW AND WHY THE PLAYS WERE WRITTEN 1

II. EARLY LIFE 47

III. CONCEALED MOTIVE 59

IV. THE PLAYS POLITICALLY GROUPED 80

V. ROMEO AND JULIET 106

VI. THE SONNETS 111

VII. THE MANUSCRIPT MYSTERY ... 134

VIII. UNOCCUPIED TIME 143

IX. JULIUS CÆSAR 146

X. CORIOLANUS 155

XI. KING HENRY VIII. 160

XII. THE TEMPEST 168

XIII. TIMON OF ATHENS 182

XIV. SUMMARY OF PROOFS 190

XV. TWELFTH NIGHT: OR, WHAT YOU WILL 217

XVI. HAMLET 260

XVII. OTHELLO 342

It is a thing indeed, if practised professionally, of low repute;
but if it be made a part of discipline, it is of excellent use:
I mean stage-playing.

BACON.

PROEM.

IF we are not yet come to question his unity, as we do that of 'the blind man of Scio's rocky isle,' an improvement in critical acuteness doubtless reserved for a distant posterity, we as little feel the power of identifying the young man who came up from Stratford, was afterwards an indifferent player in a London Theatre, and retired to his native place in middle life, with the author of *Macbeth* and *Lear*, as we can give a distinct historic personality to Homer. No letter of his writing, no record of his conversation, no character of him drawn with any fulness by a contemporary, has been produced. If there was a Shakespeare of earth, as I suspect, there was also one of heaven; and it is of him that we desire to know something.

HALLAM.

"Dramatic Poesy is as History made visible."

> BACON, *Dignity of Learning.*

"It is a kind of history."

> *Taming of the Shrew.*

"Think you see
The very persons of our noble story
As they were living."

> *King Henry 8th.*

"In this theatre of man's life it is reserved
Only for God and Angels to be lookers on."

> BACON, *Dignity of Learning.*

"A kingdom for a stage, princes to act,
And monarchs to behold the swelling scene."

> *King Henry 5th.*

"The Prince beholding
This noble action from the walls of Gaunt,
As in a theatre."

> BACON, *State Paper.*

"And stand securely on their battlements,
As in a theatre."

> *King John.*

I

HOW AND WHY THE PLAYS WERE WRITTEN.

"Thou shalt never get such a secret from me but by a parable."

"Secrets of religion,. polity, and philosophy are involved in parables."

THE political purpose of the renascence drama has never been defined. And yet for a patriotic object the series of plays so named were evidently written. The motive is avowed in prologue, epilogue, and induction; and everywhere throughout the works the aim is obvious. You are enjoined to

"think ye see
The very persons of our noble story
As they were living."

So plainly is the public end put forward that even an impromptu frolic got up on the nonce to draw mirth and moral from the winy humour of

B

a drunken egotist is no gambol, commonty, or tumbling trick, but more pleasing stuff, for

> "It is a kind of history."

And just as the mock Page checks Sly, when the sobered sot would again grovel, so does Cassius remind Brutus of the world's likeness to a theatre, when saying

> "How many ages hence
> Shall this our lofty scene be acted o'er!"

But the mimic acting should not make Cæsar merely "bleed in sport." For, addressing his compatriot, or confederate, in dramatic allegory, Cassius hints to Brutus, how their deed of blood, guilty or heroic, that to their mind, "gave their country liberty," might win approval and be repeated in shows by mimes making History visible. Both word and thought appear in the *Agamemnon.*

> "But blood that once hath flow'd,
> In purple stains of death upon the ground
> At a man's feet : who then can bid it back
> By any charm of song?
> Else him who knew to call the dead to life
> As warning unto all."

Other words and thoughts in *Macbeth* almost seem borrowed from the same play; and the graceful paraphrase of Plumptre, or the equally dramatic though more literal prose of Paley, yield examples which can be readily enough thrown into a rude heroic line.

> " The deed is done ; hear you the groaning king?
>   I struck him twice, and with two groans he dropt
>   His limbs, and stirred not from the fatal spot.
>   Now let us counsel with each other take ;
>   I would go in and charge them with the deed
>   While yet their hands still grip the gory sword."

> " A spot of blood stands on't yet unaveng'd."

> " The crafty action is the woman's part
>   In demon-spirit of ancestral crime."

> " Death-slumber is unworthy of a king."

> " Forc'd onward by fresh showers of kindred blood."

The last line is only the older way of saying :—

> " The near in blood, the nearer bloody."

Then come remorse, and the "now no more bloodshedding ;" while Ægisthus is as ready to die sword in hand, as is the bated Thane to die with harness on his back. The very porters in the two plays read their ill omens alike, when roused from their drowse in the night ; all showing how the greatest modern tragedy and the grandest tragedy of ancient Greece sound nearly alike. But, while the *Macbeth* repeats the *Agamemnon*, the Lady Gruoch, "that woman of haughty counsels," took up the rôle of a Clytemnestra or an Electra long ere translators had brought Greek fire to kindle unlettered genius.

The tragedies of Æschylos were a re-birth or *palingenesis* of Greek drama, similar to the English re-born or *renascence* drama. As inventor of the Thespian *Trilogy*, Æschylos is followed in the modern philosophic drama, where three separate themes are conjoined, to form one play, as in the combined tales and plots of *A Midsummer Night's Dream*, *Henry IV.*, and *V.*, *Cymbeline*, *Coriolanus*, and *The Tempest*. On a like threefold division Bacon drew his *Devices*, a form of dramatic composition never essayed by any other play-writer of the time. But the tripartite plan is also the general order of Bacon's method. " Nature exists in three states " is the first aphorism in the *Dignity of Learning;* and he so arranges nearly all his studies in Theology, Science, or Poetry, as in the three knowledges, Divine philosophy, Natural philosophy, and Humanity. And when he leaves the theatre, where it is not good to stay too long,— though there he finds poesy as a dream of learning, a thing sweet and varied, having in it something divine,—and entering the palace of the mind, he pays homage to the cardinal *tres in unus* of God, Nature, and Man. Then, awakening to rise above the earth, he wings his way through the clear air of philosophy, still caroling on the grand trilogy—

"And carol of thy works and wondrous ways,
Whose glory is sung as in a new song."

Descanting on the physiology of music, he shows how there "are but three percussions that create tone." For, "after every three notes, nature requireth, for all harmonical use, one half-note to be interposed," because " the sound returneth after six or after twelve," a multiple of three. The sweet odour of the musk rose or the violet fails after a third breath, nature retiring for her recuperative interval of repose, always a third part of time. Thus the poetic sage reveals the law of rhythm in melody of trilogy. Feeling how "the triplas have an agreement with the changes of motions " that "become the touches of sweet harmony," he, with a delicate and refined ear, "in his motion like an angel sings." Hence his saying, "the breath of flowers is far sweeter in the air, where it comes and goes like the warbling of music, than in the hand; therefore, nothing is more fit for that delight than to know what are the flowers and plants that best perfume the air," will remind the reader of mingled metaphors from musical sounds and perfumes of flowers in Oberon's pranks and Jessica's wooing, and show how much poetic feeling Bacon threw into his writings on natural history.

In fine, as a work of art every drama has three parts, a beginning, a middle, and an end; so has the pyramid of knowledge three stages, a basis in history, a mid part in physic, and a vertex in metaphysic, or point to which, with life short and art long, man's inquiry never may attain. The "three stages are to the depraved as the giants' hills, Pelion, Ossa, and Olympus piled upon each other," as they are piled by Hamlet when he would bury immortal agony :—

> "Now pile your dust upon the quick and dead,
> Till of this flat a mountain you have made,
> T' o'ertop old Pelion, or the skyish head
> Of blue Olympus,"

And

> "Make Ossa like a wart ; "

for thus "all things by scale ascend to unity," in prose and poetry.

With the tragic power of the Greek dramatist, the English poet rivals Menander's skill in pourtraying comic character. The double gift is shown in the dualism that creates a tragedy and a comedy for each particular theme. The peculiar feature is marked in the renascence drama, being therein unique. In the lighter tragi-comedies the two different parts are united in one play; in the purer tragedies the grander trait is kept distinct. The combined form is in *Measure for Measure, Much Ado About Nothing*, and *The Merchant of Venice;* the separate in *Macbeth* and *Pericles, Hamlet* and *The Winter's Tale.* In all these plays the plots carry out Bacon's definition of dramatic poetry as History made visible. In them all a panorama of the past shows the great ones of the present how, "both in divinity and in polity, offences of presumption are greatest;" and how none shall right their own wrong without incurring inevitable retribution. The enacted aphorisms warn them all to avoid the cardinal crimes of political or private life. Plays from History give the tragic feature of the moral; tales of romance, the comic aspect; or the two are combined in unity. Thus, Tragedy and Comedy, "framed to the life, serve for the more common commentaries of all the actions of our lives," exactly as Bacon designs. And thus also, although perhaps unwittingly, is Garrick, revivor and delineator of the duality, in a noble metaphor painted to the life, leading Tragedy and Comedy by the hand, in eloquent pictorial trilogy, and true emblem of the meaning hid beneath the speaking parable.

In dealing with political and social reforms to better human life, both the ancient and the modern reforming dramatists avow faith in the over-ruling power of a divine being. In religion, morals, politics, and poetic verve, if not quite in dramatic art, these particular ancient tragedies and comedies and the English renascence tragi-comedies agree. In a high tone conservative, they yet contemn despotism, by one ruler or by the mutable many; and Greek and English alike relate to comparable eras of intense intellectual activity, national renewal, and colonizing adventure.

Both dramatists were standing on the boundary line between two periods of culture; and the history which each places in the past is made that of his own time. Some prefer to compare the modern drama with that of Sophocles, in its finer feeling of mercy mingling with justice, rather than with the sterner rule of the elder Greek, and women who love, but never hate. The idea of the " Sweet Swan of Avon " singing to the humming " Attic Bee," were a pretty poetical conceit, with a little congruity between poetry and reality.

In as far as the modern drama deals with the world and men, and not with mythical deities, it is nearer Sophocles; but in the trilogy, *magnum loqui*, and untiring linking of guilt to punishment ever according to "the divine law of retribution," the renascence drama is all with Æschylos. His gods and goddesses love and hate in ways intensely human; the very titles of his deities are but false names in allegory; their chastisements are poetic and appropriate, and, as in the modern drama, never deferred to the world to come.

Both the ancient and the modern drama is planned upon the same rational principle; and each agrees with Bacon's definition of dramatic poetry: "Dramatic Poesy is as History made visible; for it represents actions as if they were present, whereas History represents them as past."

Illustrating the definition, Bacon continues:— "Dramatic Poesy, which has the theatre for its world, would be of excellent use if well directed; for the stage is capable of no small influence, both of discipline and of corruption. Now, of corruption in this kind we have enough; but the discipline has in our time been plainly neglected. And though in modern states play-acting is esteemed but as a toy, except when it is too satirical and biting; yet among the ancients it was used as a means of educating men's minds to virtue. Nay, it has been regarded by learned men and great philosophers as a kind of musician's bow by which men's minds may be played upon. And certainly it is most true, and one of the greatest secrets of nature, that the minds of men are more open to impressions and affections when many are gathered together than when they are alone."

"Passion, I see, is catching."

The stage had already become an arena for political conflict when the renascence drama superseded the *Miracle Play*. The newer drama came nearer home to men's business and bosoms, touching only on practical affairs, because "offences of insolency and ingratitude rarely have their doom adjourned to the world to come," a point well shown in the early draft for *Hamlet*, wherein a panting victim of bandits warns them that murder will have to be answered for at the Day of Judgment, when they mockingly reply

"What has that day to do with us?"

Retributive justice seemed too remote to exert any deterring effect on the criminal instincts, even with its certainty pitted against their hope of escaping the gibbet.   Hence the failure of *Morality* and *Miracle Play*.   They neither acted on awe nor conscience, but merely enkindled fear and superstition.

The change from the old to the new drama accompanied the Baconian definition of Dramatic Poesy.   This even Mr. Spedding cannot deny, though he doubts whether Bacon had ever heard of the renascence drama! He notes it as a "curious fact that Bacon's remarks on the character of the modern drama were probably written, and were certainly published, in the same year which saw the first collection" in the folio.   But an essentially similar definition of Representative Poetry, as a visible History, appears in the original form of the *Advancement* published in 1605, of which the form in the Latin translation of 1623 is an amplification.

To assert that Bacon had never heard of the drama is untenable from his charge against Oliver St. John, where of "Black Oliver" he says, "And for your comparisons with Richard II., I see you follow the example of them that brought him upon the stage and into print in Queen Elizabeth's time—a most prudent and admirable Queen.   But let me entreat you, that when you will speak of Queen Elizabeth or King James, you would compare them to King Henry VII. or King Edward I., or some other parallels, or by tropes or examples. There is a thing in an indictment called an innuendo; you must beware how you beckon or make signs upon the King in a dangerous sense."

The author of *Richard II.* drew tropes and parallels in a loyal way; they who put the play upon the stage were traitors.

The great incentive to reform is a clear idea of a want, with a feeling of power to supply it. To Bacon's mind reform seemed needed when he aimed to revive dramatic poetry, and, as he plainly tells, make it serve men's daily wants. He shows a mystic meaning hid beneath the fables of ancient poets, and a philosophy according to parables to be among the *desiderata* to be supplied in his *Instauration of Learning.*

Along with dramatic poetry, allegory should be defined, for it is an essential in true drama. A biographical play revives the memory of a particular career, but to live again a life must repeat itself in actual History. This is the perennial charm in the renascence drama. The past is ever being re-born, in allegory. One thing is said in words, and another in meaning. An object named represents another not named, the latter being discovered by reflection; and the play of reason and fancy in detecting analogy is a source of true delight, as it forms the educating power of dramatic poetry.

As the renascence drama these political allegories ought therefore to be known. In them natural drama is re-born, or rehabilitated. Pagan Nemesis returns to life again in the theatre, and, as a consequence, to live in the moral world. Again dramatic poetry holds a mirror up to human nature. When a deformed glass of the affections reflecting superstitious phantoms was driven from the sacred edifice, the stage became a platform to supplement the pulpit. On one the avenging principle is shown working here; in the other is heard a warning of how it will work hereafter. From the realms of fiend and deity, the new drama let poetry down to thinking, feeling, moiling daily life. Gorgons, griffins, chimeras, and myth monsters of miracle morality, gave way to the real in positive ethics. The imaginery fell before the objective. Aiming to impersonate the myth, the miracle play failed to delineate the passions. While lending bodily aspect to the soul, actual vice and virtue went unheeded. Everything on earth was directed towards a future world. But in the moral drama is no occult mode of thought. It ever turns the mystical into ridicule, the supernatural into superstition. In it and in Bacon's writings Pythagoras is always the dreamer by whose " vast and bottomless follies men have been entertained." In both is evinced equal familiarity with the Persian magic, and like ideas about Satanic aid in demonology and witchcraft. Writing on a frantic preacher, a religious madman, who implored God to keep away from the Conventicle while the fanatic prayed, Bacon says : " Yet it may have been the voice of Satan himself, put into Hacket's mouth by the evil spirit that possessed him." Amid such irreverence it would not be wonderful to find " the Devil citing Scripture for his purpose," nor the idea of it entering Bacon's head. It is precisely this that makes the Lady Constance exclaim :—

> "O Louis, stand fast ! the devil tempts thee here
> In likeness of a new-uptrimméd bride."

The evil spirit could freely possess bride or bridegroom, preacher or priest, witch or goblin :—

" Be thou a spirit of health, or goblin damn'd."

"What if it tempt you toward the flood,
  And there assume some other horrible form ? "

The author of the weird words on supernatural influence and spirits unknown, whether he were merely idly credulous or earnestly inquisitive, would be in a mood to write receipts for making witches' ointment out of the fat of children digged out of their graves; tell how the heart of " meddling monkey or busy ape," that merry, bold, witty beast, worn near man's heart, makes the wearer brave and audacious; extol the virtue of the stone worn in the toad's head; or a thousand other like freaks in natural magic, borrowed from text-writers for scientific work, or thrown into verse for drama.

Not only ought the drama to be called a renascence of the higher Greek drama, but it also is to be further styled the drama of Protestantism, inculcating as it does tenets of true piety, scorn of cant, espionage and hypocrisy, while advocating the right before might, and perfect toleration in combining the benefits of education with the blessings of religion. For the same reason, the whole Baconian philosophy is termed the Protestant organon that lets England flourish. Neither a

Brownist nor a Politician, though reared by a stern Puritan mother, many of Bacon's dearest friends were Catholic in religion. Persuasive and tolerant with everyone, preacher or priest, he, never fanatic, contemned alone seminarists of sedition. Though a leader of the Commons during the alarm at the rumoured treasons of Mary Stuart, he yet took no part in the debate that foreran her death. His silence has never been accounted for, and no one knows whether he thought her innocent or guilty. But he was privy to the thoughts of the commissioners who tried her case, and he draws her parallel in the gifted and amiable Marina.

But it must be shown that the philosopher who defines dramatic poetry is poet enough to illustrate his own definition. After explaining the principle, he with particular works fulfils its function. To prove this assertion no mere dictum it might suffice to compare the parallel writings to find them the products of one intellect, as is indeed often done unwittingly by the ablest minds in literature.

Vain and futile as it might at first seem to be to seek the elements of dramatic verse lurk-ing latent in Baconian prose, there is yet nothing visionary in the research. On every page examples abound fit to be culled in illustration. The fall of a favourite is thrown into metaphor in the words "The rotting lily is more offensive than when weeds decay," recurring in the *Sonnets :—*

"Lilies that fester smell far worse than weeds."

Play and paper again agree in motive and metaphor, and even concur in literary solecism, when in *The Advancement* it is asked—"Is not the opinion of Aristotle worthy to be regarded, wherein he saith, that young men are no fit auditors of moral philosophy, because they are not settled from the boiling heat of their affections, nor attempered with time and experience." For the passage is comparable with one in *Troilus and Cressida*, to identify thought and diction in the context with verbal error in quotation. Given to cite from memory, Bacon often quoted in mistake. The dramatist fell into like error in making Hector say—

"Not much
Unlike young men, whom Aristotle thought
Unfit to *hear moral* philosophy :
The reasons you allege do more conduce
To the hot passion of distemper'd blood
Than to make up a free determination
'Twixt right and wrong ; for pleasure and revenge
Have ears more deaf than adders to the voice
Of any true decision."

Not heeding the anachronism of Hector citing Aristotle, who lived long after him, a solecism due to the use of false names in allegory, in the liberty taken by poet or painter, it is notable that Aristotle speaks of *studying political*, not of *hearing moral* philosophy. Poet and philosopher err alike, in the same year of 1608, when both the works were published.

To explain the poet's blunder, Ulrici calls it ridicule. This might suffice for the drama, but it can afford no explanation of the error in the treatise, in which there is no sarcasm. In truth every attempt to remove the difficulty only leaves it more glaring. Thus Pope, in ascribing it to ignorance in the editors of the first Folio, says it is incredible that the error could be committed by "any man who had the least tincture of a school, or the least conversation with such as had." With all his caustic raillery, Pope yet thought Bacon the wisest and brightest of men; but Pope knew not how unbounded book lore did not prevent a blunder which he declares "must have proceeded from a man who had not so much as read any history in any book."

It is therefore clear that the author of *The Dunciad* had not over-carefully read *The Advance-*

ment of Learning! Who shall now say no new commentary is needed on the renascence drama?

In affirming that the various plays forming that grand body of dramatic literature were from time to time composed by Francis Bacon, for no commercial uses, nor ephemeral entertainment, but alone as opportune illustrations of an universal scheme of social and political philosophy, complete though never claimed, the preliminary query might be put by the incredulous thus :—Could Bacon alter his style, and adapt his phrase to suit the character of any work to which he chose to direct his gigantic powers?

That Bacon could and actually did so vary his mode in a marvellous manner while elucidating most diverse themes, is fully attested by competent judges. The erroneous belief in an unvarying style characteristic of literary composition is annihilated for ever. To illustrate this dialectic versatility, Bacon's great biographer cites many works written by Bacon, but printed in other's names. Many such *MSS.* are now in the British Museum. Some of these papers are written in, others are amended by Bacon's own hand. Several of them had been published; others have not; yet the latter were fit to be preserved, "*if not divulged;*" a secresy about which there surely hangs some mighty mystery! At any rate the time has long gone by when Bishop Lincoln's objection to publicity availed. Then "letters written *è re natâ*, and bearing a synchronism or equality of time *cum rebus gestis*," may indeed "speak the truth too plainly, and cast too glaring a light for the age wherein they were or are written." And no man had greater cause to dread exposure than the artful priest who helped to ruin Bacon with a subtle fraud. But reasons for reticence no longer exist, and truth may be known without involving compromise.

Of the papers that had evidently been composed for some masque or show, Mr. Spedding remarks :—" There is nevertheless in the style of both a certain affectation and rhetorical cadence, traceable in Bacon's other compositions of this kind, and agreeable to the taste of the time, but so alien to his own individual taste and natural manner, that there is no single feature by which his style is more plainly distinguished, wherever he speaks in his own person, whether formally or familiarly, whether in the way of narrative, argument, or oration, than the total absence of it."

Here then is proof enough of a felicitous adaptation of style as occasion required. And although no mention is here made of dramatic writings other than *Masques* and *Devices*, yet that pliant style could easily be still further varied. The idea of an immutable individuality in verbal or rhetorical style argues mean thought and paucity of matter; and the clever people who think they can detect by that criterion the hand of any author daily make great mistakes, as every anonymous writer is by personal experience well aware. And hence, when Queen Elizabeth vowed that a seditious book was never his whose name was to it, but some more mischievous traitor's, and would have him racked to tell who was the real author, Bacon said to her not to rack his person, but rack his style, he merely played upon a very vulgar error, to evade with harmless equivoke a rather tender point. For the Queen was wroth at treason, and Bacon allayed her fears, for Essex' sake, whose cause he was earnestly pleading. Even Mr. Spedding admits that wherever a literary doubt has to be decided by the test of style, "the reader must be allowed to judge for himself." He accordingly now trusts more to the matter than the manner; and therefore follows Bacon's rule, that because poetry is a part of learning in measure of words for the most part restrained, but in all other points free and licensed, and referred to the Imagination, which may at pleasure make unlawful matches and divorces of things, is taken in two senses; in respect of words and matter. In the first sense it is but a character of speech; for verse is only a kind of style, and has nothing to do with the matter. True history may be written in verse, and feigned history in prose. True poetry is feigned history. "That Bacon was an adept at the accomplished letter writer's art of suiting his style to his correspondents," is now allowed by *The Edinburgh Review*. All the classic quotations in the *Dignity of Learning* are turned by Mr. Spedding freely into English heroic numbers. That the bold and figurative rhetoric with which Bacon charms his reader can be readily thrown into heroic verse, conclusive proof was given when the writer playfully threw many parts into that form, and showed them to literary people who, after vainly hunting through all the concordances, concluded that the magically turned sentences must be "some old readings." The pleasantry may not be again attempted. A dainty bit is " Honey of Hybla," as Bacon observes, and Prince Henry repeats.

" The meat is sav'ry when the stomach 's good."

If this transmuting could be cunningly enough done by one who does not profess to be a poet, and little reads poetry, how infinitely more freely could quaint prose be charmed into sparkling verse by him who had, to Hallam's mind, "the poetic faculty in the highest degree"? Facile indeed would the art of conversion be to him in whom Macaulay perceives the gift of word play without art "developed almost to a disease;" who inspires Addison to "talk with rapture of his beautiful lights, graces, and embellishments;" and of whom the enthusiastic Taine vows "he thought in the manner of artists and poets," uttering thought "by poetical figures, by enigmatic abbreviations, almost in Sibylline verses. Shakespeare and the seers do not contain more vigorous or expressive condensations of thought, more resembling inspiration, and in Bacon they are found everywhere. His process is that of the creators; it is intuition, not reasoning. Than his diction, nothing is finer in the English tongue."

To the still more minutely analytic and poetic, or creative mind of Goethe, the plays of the renascence drama seem "as if they were performances of some celestial genius, descending among men, to make them, by the simplest instruction, acquainted with themselves.   They are no fictions."

These words of Goethe convey the same ideal of the poet that corresponding words of Taine convey regarding the philosopher, in almost literally identical panegyric.   Both Goethe and Taine are gifted interpreters of æsthetic feeling, and recondite explorers of the outward source of inward emotion. Both write subjectively on the effect produced by the works of two supposed different authors.   In each the "whole soul is in commotion" to express the psychic perturbation in the same impressive words.   Does not one and the same effluence operate on the genial sympathies of both ?   In perfect harmony of opinion with Macaulay, after that exacting master exhausts his repertory of attack, they agree with him that the object of his magnificent vituperation still had "the most exquisitely constructed intellect that has ever been bestowed on any of the children of men."   Willingly would they don the garb in which the faithful editor's graceful imagery more finely clothes their noble conception of the mind

> " Whose even threads the Fates spin round and full
> Out of their choicest and their whitest wool."

For doth not rare Ben extol Bacon as " He who hath filled up all numbers, and performed that in our tongue, which may be compared or preferred either to ancient Greece, or haughty Rome. In short, within his view, and about his times, were all wits born, that could honour a language, or help study. Now things daily fall, wits grow downward, and eloquence grows backward: so that he may be named and stand as the *àkmñ* of our language." No pinnacle has two acmes, and Jonson's *Scriptorum Catalogus* points high to the one peerless name.

And just as Campbell's bitter invective admits Bacon " more than any man that ever lived could mix refined speculation with grovelling occupations;." or Spedding's chaster eulogy avers "he could imagine like a poet and execute like a clerk of works;" or Osborne's graphic gossip says "he could talk with a country lord about dogs and hawks, and next minute outcant a London chirurgeon;" so will the poet's mind soar in speculative thought or work in thrifty handicraft. His own aim was for "a discovery of observations from immortality (if it were possible) to the meanest mechanical practice." With his own hand Bacon could stuff a dead fowl with snow precisely as would Lord Cerimon. Allowed by all to be the wisest and brightest of men, whether he also was "meanest" would not, even if proved as it is not, touch the question of dramatic power. Mr. Hallam, who well knew what it is to be wise, great, and good, is content to say "Bacon, 'the wisest, greatest of mankind.'"

As Bacon's style is wanton in word-play, so are the compared poems full of "conceits and quibbles," that "play'd with words to please a quibbling age." Reveling in mirth, fun, and word frolic, they "rhyme you eight years together, either in the true or false gallop of verses." Equally so was he, who did not profess to be a poet, often enough reminded of his poetical conceits. He vowed to be ever a stranger to poets, and openly abjured them to evade the ill word of rivals who told the Queen that he, the great reader, writer, and thinker, was unfit for practical affairs. The vulgar opinion bred in envy is confuted by his practical sagacity. Active talent and love of letters are never incompatible ; one rather quickens the other's efficiency. To poesy

Bacon freely ascribes that which is its due. "For the expressing of affections, passions, corruptions, and customs, we are beholding to poets more than to philosophers' works; and for wit and eloquence not much less than to orators' harangues. But it is not good to stay too long in the theatre." If he then would thus quickly pass on to the judicial place or palace of the mind with reverence and attention, it is entirely because in the third part of learning he can find no deficience. The most adroit monarch that ever reigned longed to be a Princess by poetry somehow-made immortal. Of her the ignorant poet said, "For the beauty and many graces of her presence, what colours are fine enough for such a portraiture? Let no light poet be used for such a description, but the chastest and the royalest." Adding that "the monuments of wit survive the monuments of power: the verses of the poet endure, without a syllable lost, while states and empires fade," words surely allied to their counterpart in the following lines from the *Sonnets*:—

> "Not marble, nor the gilded monuments
> Of princes, shall outlive this powerful rhyme."

The imagery in prose and verse compel belief in one origin, a duality perceived by Donne, who declares Bacon to be "a man so rare in knowledge of so many several kinds, endued with the facility and felicity of expressing it all, in so elegant, significant, so abundant, and yet so choice and ravishing a way of words, of metaphors, and allusions, as perhaps the world hath not seen since it was a world." The doctor fears his ardent eulogy "may seem a great hyperbole, and strange kind of riotous excess of speech." But Dr. Donne offers a fair challenge. " The best means of putting me to shame will be, for you to place any other man of yours by this of mine. And this little makes a shift to show that the genius of England is still not only eminent, but predominant, for the assembling great variety of those rare parts, in some single man, which use to be half incompatible anywhere else." Or, as Dr. Rawley puts it : "Abilities which commonly go single in other men are all conjoined in him"—"Two glasses, such as certainly the like never met in one age."

After this eulogium by a thoughtful, delightful poet after old Izaac Walton's own heart, it can no longer be deemed hyperbole in the biographer to infer from one sample "that Bacon had all the natural faculties which a poet wants ; a fine ear for metre, a fine feeling for imaginative effect in words, and a vein of poetic passion ;" or declare of another verse that "the thought could not well be fitted with imagery words and rhythm more apt and imaginative, in a tenderness of expression which manifestly comes from the heart in sensitive sympathy with nature, and fully capable of the poet's faith,

'That every flower enjoys the air it breathes.'"

"The breath of flowers" made Bacon think they breathe. Of a third verse Mr. Spedding says "the heroic couplet could hardly do its work better in the hands of Dryden." All Bacon's quotations from the ancient poets are turned by Mr. Spedding into English heroic verse, and therefore Bacon could have done that for himself had he thought fit.

Here then are unqualified proofs of a thorough belief in a devoted student, that "Bacon was not without the 'fine phrensy' of the poet ;" and that when the divine afflatus rose in "the ordinary direction, it carried him to a place among the great poets." Nor can this be called the biased view of a partial editor, for it concurs with what Hallam says on citing a remark by Dugald Stewart, that "in one short but beautiful paragraph concerning *Poetry*, he has exhausted everything that philosophy and good sense have yet had to offer, on what has been since

called the *Beau Ideal.*" Along with this passage
Stewart used the phrase "mysticism in the *cloud-
capt* metaphysics," as if he thought of "the cloud-
capt towers," rising in the most gorgeous image in
poetry.

Although verses were vowed out of Bacon's
line, the study of his life being "to refrain his
imagination," the laws of which he studied with
peculiar care, he yet confesses to have once written
a *Sonnet,* "meant in some way or other to sweeten
the Queen's temper towards the Earl of Essex;"
but that poem "has either not been preserved at all,
or not so as to be identified." Never identified;
and yet Lord Campbell sneers at its merit! He,
like Hume, Pope, and a thousand more, sneer at
what they never read. But identification will come
in due time. Meanwhile the admissions show how
able men perceive in the works of Bacon indications
of a mind gifted with the highest poetic power;
and, if "what Milton said of Shakespeare—

> 'That each heart
> Hath from the leaves of thy unvalu'd book
> Those Delphic lines with deep impression took'—

may as truly be said of Bacon," then must Bacon
have been equally capable of writing the renascence

drama.   Other writings are traced through internal evidence to him as their author, and why should not the drama be submitted to a similar ordeal?   " It was," remarks Mr. Spedding, " owing to the *style* (which has a strong character of its own, quite unlike Bacon's) that I was myself first led, in spite of the signature, to question the authorship.   But when I came to examine the sense, and understand the allusions, I found the matter still more conclusive than the style."   Still further applying the same criterion will merely enlarge the induction.   Metrical tests, counted words, weak or feminine endings, balanced rhymes, and repetitions may afford an inkling of the method and imagination of the playwright; but of the authorship of the drama those merely verbal tests reveal nothing.   The criterion of identity may be carried further to show that excellent critics ever unconsciously ascribe to one author attributes claimed for the other.   The *Saturday Review* says Bacon " clothed his thoughts in terse, vigorous, and vivid language, such as commends them to the imagination, and sets him side by side with Shakespeare in the memory of his countrymen."   This " coiner of fine phrases " incensed Mr. Huxley, by saying of Dr. Gilbert that a whole system of philosophy cannot come out of a magnet. . While a reason once is a reason ever; yet, too wide generalizing is an· idol of the laboratory. But, Gilbert is not ignored. He is "excellently"— *optime notavit*—named in the discourse on the new-found "motion to the earth's centre." This motion is an appetite of bodies, like Cressida's heart, "drawing all things to it." The reference occurs in the *Intellectual Globe*, which Mr. Huxley, who has "read his leaf," has probably met with. If the coiner of fine phrases did nothing more than call the wits together, neither "are we the richer by one poor invention" of his censor. If Bacon did endow and adorn thought with speech, he also knew well that "knowledge itself is more beautiful than any apparel of words that can be put upon it." In finding "the things which have forbidden the happy match between the mind of man and the nature of things," the Great Natural Philosopher clearly defined Man's place in Nature. And, moreover, if Huxley did justly vindicate vivisection, hateful and inhuman as it is, from the unfair aspersions of mere sentimental humanitarians, the modern protagonist did no more than follow in the wake of the prototype. For does not Bacon also contend for the right to study anatomy in the living subject, that "utility may be considered as well as humanity"?

But, in employing comparative anatomy or therapeutics, as he often recommended, Bacon would sanction no idle cruelty, or wanton trial. His true feeling is spoken in the colloquy between the Queen and Doctor Cornelius, in *Cymbeline.*

> " I will try the forces
> Of these thy compounds on such creatures as
> We count not worth the hanging, (but none human),
> To try the vigour of them, and apply
> Allayments to their act ; and by them gather
> Their several virtues and effects."

> " Your highness
> Shall from this practice but make hard your heart:
> Besides, the seeing these effects will be
> Both noisome and infectious."

These lines express Bacon's views humane and philosophic on experiments on "all sorts of beasts, for dissections and trials," to learn "what may be wrought upon the body of man ; we try also all poisons and other medicines upon them."

It is true that Bacon gave an exposition of the then accepted doctrine of spontaneous generation. But his brief outline of that hypothesis appeared before Redi tried the crucial experiment which Bacon had directed, and caught his death

from cold hands in conducting. Had he but lived
a little while to know the happy outcome of his
first trial of the freezing process for preserving
meat, success would have led him to elucidate
the whole reason of the "moss that comes
between putrefaction and a plant," a subject that
has taken nigh three centuries to perfite. For
have not Needham, and Pouchet, and Bastian, since
aimed to confute Spallanzani, who was Redi's great
supporter? And do not even now many brave
biologists, with Bastian, maintain that common
fevers, which depend for their cause on germs,
or seeds, or living organisms, arise *de novo* in seeth-
ing mud, as alligators were aforetime devoutly
thought to originate "as a plant which comes
from the lust of the earth without a formal seed."
And when the doughty Tyndall mocked at his
opponent Bastian's fine "effluence of words," did
not the verbally eloquent protospermist but vainly
try to emulate the flouted philosopher's saying
that in transcendentals "men aimed rather at
height of speech than of the subtleties of things"?
Wherefore Bacon wished "the real and solid
inquiry, according to the laws of Nature, and not
of language."

Coining no fine phrases about mystic "archebiosis," equivocal "abiogenesis," or profound "Bathybius"—"a common parent, like unto Berecynthia, who had so much heavenly issue"—dream terms that like *idola* of the laboratory vanished in a decade to join the vagaries of Lucretius, which they imitated, Bacon's clear, crisp, pure English led to the enduring, because he "with reason set down as deficient" knowledge of the facts of Nature. Not pretending to know the unknown, Bacon proposed the method of trial, which Redi followed, and brought proof out of physical demonstration for plainly phrased philosophy. There is a marked resemblance between Bacon's idea of seed springing from the lust of the earth, and maggots bred of the sun "Being a god kissing carrion." With this knowledge before them, puzzled commenters need never have been baffled in attempting to interpret Hamlet's words. So, in

> "These summer-flies
> Have blown me full of maggot ostentation,"

is a suggestive phrase that may have led Redi, after reading Bacon's views, to try the experiment that finally proved the truth.

In the new edition of the *Novum Organum* Mr. Fowler alludes to "the marvellous language in which Bacon clothes his thoughts." His utterances are not infrequently marked with a grandeur and solemnity of tone, a majesty of diction, which renders it impossible to criticise them. There is no author, unless it be Shakespeare, who is so easily remembered or so frequently quoted. There is a something about Bacon's diction, his quaintness of expression, and his power of illustration, which lays hold of the mind, and lodges itself in the memory, in a way which we hardly find paralleled in any other author, except it be Shakespeare."

The prayer written in the hour of humiliation "reads like the sighing of an angel," and is "the finest bit of composition in the English tongue." His last *will* contains many passages of "real pathos and sublimity." His "words and thoughts are interwoven in our mother tongue."

Such are the appreciative utterances of men themselves masters in English composition, many of them versatile in genius and of intellectual grandeur.

In like manner Gladstone and Dowden perceive a terrene spirit pervade both sets of writings, proving kinship in worldly thought, if not equally in religious feeling. Newton liked not the plays for they prove nothing; to him the poet was not mathematical; and geometry showed Bacon's one intellectual defect. On a weak point the *Intellectual Globe* and the *Drama* are at one.

When, in 1603, Chettle wrote *Englandes Mourning Garment*, he chid "silver-tongèd Melicert" for forgetting the memory of the late Queen, by not letting

"Drop from his honied muse one sable teare."

But censuring Chettle was not aware that after the Essex affair high silence reigned between Elizabeth and Bacon, unbroken to the end of her days, and that this was the secret of the tearless muse by Chettle lamented.

The poet Campbell commends the drama for deep insight into human motive unavowed, but only as it is discernible through human action, for he finds him "reading Macbeth's character in a way such as Bacon could not have given to us more philosophically, or in fewer words." He indeed could not do more. And on points of identity Campbell's idea agrees with Walpole's, as expressed in the *Historic Doubts*, wherein it is shown that Poet and Historian wrote alike on Richard III., Henry VII., and Perkin Warbeck, the pretended heir to the throne, who was supposed to have been smothered in the Tower.

With this opinion of a common authorship of these several works any candid reader will agree who can take the trouble to read over the last scene in *Richard III.*, and then peruse the opening paragraph of *Henry VII.;* for then it will be found that the latter is a brief recapitulation by the historian who, after finishing in drama the history of one great era, reviews what he taught by way of introducing the new historical lesson to follow.

After Sir Thomas More, to drama and history are due the general notion entertained about those three personages and the events associated with their lives. The poetical and the historical versions not only agree, but, according to the later researches of Mr. Gairdner, they are the true chronicles. The fallen Chancellor is roundly accused of writing the dramatic *History of Henry VII.* to flatter the regal vanity of King James, and praise a living Stuart at the expense of a dead Plantagenet. But the poet is similarly blamed for writing *Richard III.* to gratify Elizabeth Tudor, in whose veins and James's ran the same strain of blood. In thus attributing a like motive to dramatist and historian, men's thoughts unwittingly still dwell on their identity. And this, too, even although the historian's tribute of respect is reviled as abject and servile, while the pæan of the favoured poet is euphemistically extolled as loyal eulogy, craven meanness in one, becoming chivalry in the other, for "the same crime is rewarded in one man with a gibbet, and in another with a crown." And if, as Walpole holds, and all will agree, *A Winter's Tale* was written to please Elizabeth, by clearing her mother's repute against her father's defaming as

> "A gracious innocent soul,
> More free than he is jealous,"

then was the politic dramatist, like the political historian, just such another subtle courtier. However the character of the Henry VIII. of history may be viewed is nothing to the present argument, which only goes to prove that the opinions given in the drama and in Bacon's writings agree. In the *Fortunate Memory of Elizabeth* a reference to the fact that the fate of her mother did not mar the dignity of her birth, to the criminal charge against her, and to the memorable words spoken with a high spirit in protestation of innocence, are all suggestive of Hermione as her parallel; the nearer so if taken along with the words of Anne Boleyn in the play of *Henry VIII.* An accurate idea of the real author of the drama removes all doubt about the meaning of these two plays.

Thus, when Mr. Spedding is at a loss to explain the striking likeness between Perdita's list of flowers in *A Winter's Tale*, with the list given in Bacon's *Essay of Gardens*, he admits that "if this essay had been contained in the earlier edition" he would have thought the nominal dramatist had been reading it. But as the essay was not published till 1625, nine years after the worthy's death, this could not be, unless the work was read in manuscript. On the other hand, since the drama was published in 1623, the essayist might have read it; or, perhaps poet and essayist wrote together on flowers alike. The dates of publication for drama and essay are known; but not the period of their composition. That one wrote both is the daintier riddle.

The flower naming here noted as alike in essay and drama is a mere naming and no more, a flower grower's gardening calendar. But the parity goes nearer in the entwining flowers with music to regale both senses. The colouring of tune, tints of flowers, soft touch of velvet rose leaf where sits the bee to suck honey, are all brought together to give delight in natural harmony. When Perdita tells Florizel about

> "Lilies of all kinds,
> The flower-de-luce being one,"

the artless maid repeats idle jotting in a rough diary on a "fyne border set with flagges of all sorts of flower-de-luce and lylyes." And again, "so singular in each particular" are the pair, when Oberon sings of

> "A bank whereon the wild thyme blows,
> Where ox-lips and the nodding violet grows;
> Quite over-canopied with luscious woodbine,
> With sweet musk-roses, and with eglantine,"

the chanting fairy king recalls some charmingly innocent notes about a fair plot to turn into a place of pleasure, with a fine little stream rippling over gravel on a pebble bottom, round an island, with the bank turfed, a walk, a lake, a fair row of images round, and flowers, especially violets and strawberries, an island where the fair hornbeam stands, with a rock, a grot, every island with a fair image to keep it, Tryten or Nymphe, an island with an arbour of musk-roses, set with double violets for scent in autumn, some gilovers which likewise disperse scent, and a fair bridge to the middle island only, the rest by boat.

Now, while it would need poetic feeling to fancy the rill, lake, flowery glade, walks, moon-beams flickering on the ripple on the wave like quaver in music or figure in rhetoric, all mingling on a bank to play upon, enough to wrap a young poet and Platonic lover in a midsummer night's dream over "a fair vestal thronèd by the west;" or imagine how he thereon

> "Might see young Cupid's fiery shaft
> Quench'd in the chaste beams of the watery moon,
> And the imperial votaress passing on
> In maiden meditation, fancy free,"—

a veritable Perdita, whose loveable mother, Anne Boleyn, was believed by the poet innocent; yet, in the double picture there are three objects for matter-of-fact logic. There is first the particular flowers preferred, along with the peculiarly endearing way of naming them; second, the mode of combining flowers, scents, colours, sculptures, rills, music, and moonbeams playing on the water to heighten all the feelings; and third, the like ideas on the loves of plants and methods of meliorating so delicately hinted at by Perdita and dwelt upon by Bacon. For, when he alludes to the art of varying fruits and flowers that grafting cannot give, he yet shows how the stock must be inferior to the scion, for the scion will govern; and so

> "You see, sweet maid, we marry
> A gentler scion to the wildest stock,
> And make conceive a bark of baser kind
> By bud of nobler race."

When Bacon names thyme he ever calls it the "wild thyme;" and he takes infinite pains to explain the natural cause of the inclining and bending of the "nodding" violet. On the various ways of propagating plants by slips, buds on bark, engrafting, inocculating to breed bastards, hybrids, or streaked gillyvors, of toadstools and moss, he is all replete with what may well be termed the raw material of poetic conceits deftly inwrought by cunning of high art to appear playful in drama. For it would need no more wit to turn his prose upon flowers into verse about gardens, than it would take to convert his ideal "girdle of the world" into Puck's "girdle round about the earth." The flowers have all been catalogued and compared by Mr. Spedding, who has not, however, ventured to name them along with other delights, either to convey unthought of charm, or reveal the undoubted charmer.

It may be urged that those *notes* were writ in 1608, while the play appeared long before. But as they were transfers from earlier scrap-books, their date cannot be learned. Nor can it be believed that Bacon never dreamt of so adorning his home until prompted by wealth. It was the idol of his life. And in 1590, the date as near as may be of the *Midsummer Night's Dream* trilogy, Bacon adored the maiden Queen, and never let slip an opportunity of paying her neat compliment, chaste, with no flattery.

Finally, Dr. Abbott, impelled by the scholastic function, indites a treatise "to furnish students of Shakespeare and Bacon with a short systematic account" of their peculiar syntax. The two series of writings supply the grammarian with all the examples required for their mutual illustration. Taken together they form an unique body of language, differing from the common idiom. In expounding the poet by the philosopher, and the philosopher by the poet, the works are found to reciprocate. It is the same with Aldis Wright, who, like Ben Jonson, edited the *First Folio* along with *The Advancement*, as if the pair were inseparable.

This effort of Dr. Abbott to identify the syntax in the two sets of works makes the question of their common authorship to be no longer a mere matter of idle speculation, but one radically affecting the philology of that form of the English tongue which has been found by experience the best exponent of English thought.

Finally, when alluding to the only specimen we have of Bacon's felicity in dialogue, Mr. Spedding, regarding the work as a literary composition, says enough is done in it to show how skilfully he could handle that fine but difficult instrument; and that with the spectators bringing in the full force of their wit and learning, nothing can be more natural and life-like than their conversation, possessing as it does an animation which forms the very essence of dramatic writing.

Here then is all throughout a marvellous consensus of opinion on the likeness of the writings of Bacon to the renascence drama, as if mind and art were felt to be the same.   When critic and commentator do agree their unanimity is wonderful. To one of the earlier printed plays good Mr. Mathews did after all probably refer when telling his friend he had got a little book of his, "only known under another name."   The secret of that name confided to Mathews would be sacred.

To gather into one bundle a few hanks showing where a poet's lays and a philosopher's works are spun off one distaff is the aim of the new life-thread, with "a knot on the thrid, not to lose the stitch." If "a thrid of mine own life" be fairly run out, the clew will leave no loop or kink in line of proof that the two wind and twine into one glory for literature. And may the weaver, with life flying like his own shuttle, invoke

> "O Fates, come, come,
> Cut thread and thrum,"

if, in spinning a mingled yarn round and full out of their own softest and whitest wool, the thrower "draweth out the thread of his verbosity finer than the staple of his argument!"

II

EARLY LIFE.

"Thou art thy mother's glass."

"He took mind and feature from his mother."

HAVING thus found Bacon well endowed by nature with the poetic faculty, it will next be shown how he daily learned truths new and old, without a familiar knowledge of which the re-born drama could never have been written. A few of the abounding classical allusions in the dialogue, that serve as Attic salt or sallet herbs to season discourse, might have come from sources other than original; but the vast array of acquired learning employed in constructing the drama is as far beyond the range of mean abridgments, that Bacon despised, as it is without the pale of the imaginable; while very many salient facts in it literally belong to Bacon's private history. Born in 1560, the youth gave early token of the future paragon. Before his tenth year his mind like his head and face had been subjects of psychological study. The very painter who drew his portrait wished "that one could also paint his mind," one being then as now an index to the other. A fine intelligent lad one day seeing the portrait said, "O, I should not like to have a head like that;" and truly it is to older heads a kind of puzzle, for none can at the first look tell whether it is a likeness of boy or woman. The massive head is curved by the arch of a pure cycloid, rising from a full brow and temple over a deep-set eye looking out into everything for thoughts that the long eloquent upper lip is ready to utter, unless restrained to wise reticence by the quiet thin waving nether lip and round chin keeping guard at the portal of speech.

At his mother's knee Bacon learned to be like her a linguist, while an Italian tutor taught him the language of his country, and made him familiar with a romance literature afterwards interwoven into the pattern and fabric of the drama. The tales and novels then very little known in England were among the playthings of his boyhood. Merry, witty, apt, genial, gentle, and diffident, his homely pastimes nurtured his native disposition. He never went to school, but when very young entered the university. There the juvenile reformer could not brook the despotism of professors; he must think, and in thinking doubt the virtue of a logic that only made men too disputable for his company. He even then thought of as many things as they did, but he thanked God and said nothing. Throughout life, and during a long career of earnest research for altering the bases of science and philosophy, he never was didactic, but ever would rather inquire than argue. A great speaker in debate, he yet was no talker tiring with garrulity, and he would only reiterate for deeper question, "to delve him to the root," as he "with the sharp edge of my words will delve to the root of the matter." What he called "a Greek invocation to call fools into a circle" made him before eighteen resolve to reform science for practical uses. The rhetoric of schoolmen was a sharp weapon for the casuist to wield, but was not an instrument in any way useful for exploring nature. The Stagyrite fallacy bred disputation in religion and hindered progress in science; but of two great books or volumes open to him, the Scriptures and the Book of Nature, Bacon read one in simple confiding faith, the other he read to know it, and find therein sermons in stones and good in everything; knowledge not to be got without diligent reading unless by one "somewhat supernatural and divine," qualities to which he made no pretension. He was no *ontologist*, seeking to know the nature and will of God; for he contentedly only sought after an useful knowledge in interpreting Nature. Hence many declare him no philosopher, but only, in the schoolmen's sense, a logician. As a lover of practical wisdom he opened a fountain of natural knowledge, and men at length begin to discern whence the issues, and where the streams thereof now take and fall.

, Leaving the academy where the lava of ancient lore lay congealed in scholastic systems, unbroken into elements of new fertility, he went over when barely eighteen to France, where he associated with learned men and women, and was friendly and intimately familiar with all who were renowned among a refined court and cultured people.   There, surveying the state of Europe, he studied foreign policy along with the ephemeral ways of courtiers and the far-reaching plans of philosophic politicians.   Insight gained in a high school of statecraft set deeply into a retentive mind, to well out again in "the drama for kings and statesmen."   To him

"The court 's a learning-place,"

for such conversation as that which opens *Cymbeline ;* or in the idiomatic French chat in the courtship of *Henry V.*, so racy of the soil that doubting critics think some native helped a poet who needed no aid.   A rich repeating memory put into others' mouths words that had often entered his own ears.   Ever on the alert to make all knowledge his province, to serve the scheme of his new philosophy, he would when sailing on the Channel attend to the jargon of a ship's crew handling a man-of-war at sea, and be able to repeat their sea slang to the wonder of nautical experts and to the astonishment of landsmen.   During four trips across, twice going and twice returning, the youngster, remarkable for quickness and sagacity, had ample time and opportunity to learn the deftest way to work a ship through a storm, or a wreck in a tempest, or to describe the *Great Harry* he sailed in, or any ship of 1100 tons, as he does in the *History of Winds*, with fair and full detail on hull, gear, spars, sails, rope, cordage, and tackling, so as to make folk fancy he borrowed from Italian writers on naval architecture. But the author so, in their minds, copied, is as great an enigma to those who do not think Bacon original, as are the novels embodied in the plays. There need hence be no more marvel over the accurate nautical knowledge in the drama, or at phraseology that fell on ears or sights on the eyes of a lad never bird-witted, but ever attentive to look and listen. How he acquired technical knowledge in medicine and in music will presently appear, it being enough now to say that he had direct information in both professions, arts, or sciences.

His father's sudden death made young Francis return from Paris to London in 1580, to face the world as a youth of twenty, without patrimony, office, or bread-winning calling. He was named to the Queen as a rare youth for her help, though no good word was needed to remind her of the gravity and maturity above his years of her own "young lord-keeper." The way for him was never barred by her, but was closed only by his own potent relative, the elder Cecil, who thought his studious nephew of a fine wit, but too much a reader and thinker for routine toil, unlikely to be a tool to govern with, or an accessible spy for state utility. Therefore the "my poor suit" of the bashful applicant was rejected; and because his head was full of mighty projects with which practical men had no immediate sympathy, his purse was left empty. Without an opening even for humble toil, and being no longer able to live to study, as wise folk say he should have done in a hermitage at Cambridge, he had to contrive to live amid the bustle of London. Through the means got by "a lively imagination guiding a ready pen," he entered an ungenial guild for earning a precarious income; but "the trade whereto he was born" was neither to his liking nor his hope, and he often did with fortune chide,

> "That did not better for my life provide,"

than a calling that made his nature almost like a dyer's hand, subdued to what he worked in, which foes misused for inclination.

But the moiling attorney never let sleep his pre-vision of the outcome from the state of England, pregnant with a grand future. That future he foresaw as vividly as he in later days clearly descried the Salomon's House now at last reared after three centuries in our fairly built city, fit Bensalem for the Happy Land of that prophetic dream. Forethought and Fable find their prototype in Melbourne, and have become reality, even in the unknown territory of *The New Atlantis*.

While longing to reform science for all men, he for the Queen would ever be ready to do what he never would do for his own gain. In her service his mind turned on other wheels than those of profit, and a diary meant for no eye save his own reveals the pure, unselfish, high-minded, patriotic motive. Amid a gay throng of gainly Blounts and "dancing Hattons," noble animals, lithe of limb, quiet Francis was the only young favourite chosen for intellect alone. Scandal never breathed his name as a mate of fortune or of adventure for exotic royalty in Platonic lovemaking. He looked with awe on the Queen as the Princess in the blessed islands, who only permitted amorous admiration. The implied preference for exalted intellect was fraught with good for sovereign and subject, guiding as it did their future happy destiny.

The prudent stateswoman, ever on the look-out for wit and wisdom in counsel, and whistling for the ablest men, clave to him, and would often train him on to hear his opinion on public polity. Devoted to her cause from childhood, from early training and matured conviction, he became her "ignorant statesman," abler to guide because only a looker-on, as he himself explains. As volunteer he advised on great issues. The famed letter of advice to the Queen eventually became so important that it "was set down, to give it greater authority, as the production of her most famous counsellor." But, it is evidently the production of some young unauthorized adviser, who feels it necessary to offer an apology for volunteering his advice. It is described as a letter of advice to Queen Elizabeth, touching the course to be taken for protection against her enemies at home and abroad; and was probably written about the end of 1584, very nearly the period when the earliest draft of *Hamlet* is now found to have been written. Following not long after that notable letter came the even more dramatic *Discourse in Praise of the Queen*, and the many rare traits of verbal and ideal likeness between those two works and the *Twelfth Night* are so near and fine that a comparison of the three will yield a prelude to the argument for a common authorship, a *Filum Labyrinthi* or thread leading into the long-hidden closet where will be found proof that letter, discourse, and drama had one mind, one tongue, one pen, for their production. That these works were written to convey to the Queen hints for her guidance is corroborated by Bacon's habit of advising friends, Essex, Mathews, Villiers, and others, and especially the King, on the union of the kingdoms, on Church matters, revision of the Scriptures, and so forth; modes of admonishing which brought upon him hateful names for that "meannes" for which he still is unworthily reviled.

In addition to this brief and cursory outline compiled from oft-related narratives of incidents that shaped Bacon's after-life, rough hew it how he would, and their close relation to the drama, further reference to the biography of his later years will be connected with the particular plays of their respective periods. Meanwhile it will now suffice to add that between 1609, when he was first installed into active official life, and 1621, after conspiracy betrayed and overthrew him, and ingratitude left him, without infamy beyond a vague assent to avoid strained to admission of guilt, in the depth of penury to want and ignominy, and as before 1609, with little save literary work to do, no new plays are *known* to have been written. In that long interval none were printed, or known to be in the hand of player or printer, leaving the dates of production of a dozen to be accounted for by conjecture from collateral evidence, no two guessers agreeing in their chronology. Nor is inquiry helped by a single incident in the career of the putative poet who lived in London three years after 1609; neither is it aided by the doings of his fellows who remained about their theatre for several years longer, unheard of until Ben Jonson employed them to bring out the 1623 Folio, of which he was undoubtedly real editor, they as practical players helping him to divide the text, written running, into acts and scenes adapted for an improved stage carpentery. And so will vain conjecture ever differ until discourse of reason reconcile imaginary fact, unreal thinking, and idle guessing, to Bacon's political labour and the evolution of the colossal empire with which his avowed works and the renascence drama are alike inseparably linked.

III

CONCEALED MOTIVE.

"The glory of GOD is to conceal a thing, but the glory of the King is to find it out."

"I hold it the more knavery to conceal, and therein am I constant to my profession."

WHEN Autolycus avoids inquiring people with a cheery tongue, he, a "courtier cap-a-piè," holds it no knavery to conceal court enfoldings from vulgar ken; nor was the palace pedlar the only courtier of the time who could adroitly conceal a fatal court enfolding with a pleasantry. On every variety of court enfolding was Bacon daily employed writing in others' names; and, if "we do not think the worse of Plato for personating Socrates, or of Cicero for personating Cato," neither should ill be thought of Bacon for borrowing a name to cover his aim from those who might not care for his roundabout way of working for "the benefit and relief of the state of society and man," and quietly "do something for the good of men's souls, the state of religion being such" as to need a monitor like that found in the drama. In troubled times patriots and philanthropists often resorted to the same expedient for safety; even brave John Rogers himself dare only print his Tindale's *Bible* under the fictitious name of one Thomas Mathews, as he did without thinking about either fraud or falsehood. Gallows and knock were too powerful in that way; beating and hanging were terrors to him; for the life to come, he slept out the thought of it; not that he feared the stake for his own flesh, but he would not have his precious *Book* burned. That volume Bacon often read; and on a shelf in Melbourne Public Library rests a copy that may hold the finger-mark he made as he learned from his mother all about the borrowed title, and got therefrom a hint for his own drama. Such cautelous device was needed in those days in printing innovating books, that had the real author of *Richard II.* revealed his name and avowed his work on the eve of the Essex rising, when the play was acted overnight by rebels who perverted the poet's trope to foster their sedition and embolden their followers in the morning, his hapless neck would quickly have dropt between axe and block for his temerity,. as a fine stroke in revenge by "blow for blow" Southampton, inciter, ringleader, approver. The hope of gaining greater good to society from indirect than from open political agitation explains the reticence of one who was ruined by it eventually, because unwilling to make known his method even in the *Interpretation of Nature;* for that work was printed under the fictitious title of *Valernis Terminus*, with notes by "Hermes Stella," to veil the newly-inculcated doctrine in an obscure style, and let the work find readers worthy of having conveyed to them the. hidden meaning. Borrowing a title for the drama was thus in keeping with all that Bacon did; and yet, as Spedding observes, "There are some persons who hold it a kind of heresy to question the authorship of anything which has been printed as authentic in a book of good repute;" but the biographer is not of that way of thinking, he knowing well how Bacon and many other good men then living in harried England did "by design dissemble for honourable commonwealth courses." In reviving old Greek drama for new general learning Bacon dreamt of no harm in veiling his name. He knew how dangling creatures hanging on the wink of princes could get rid of him and his allegory, to defeat his proposed reform. If what he wrote got a hearing, little cared he for notoriety as author; and nobody calls Burghley, Essex, Walsingham, or Herbert either wicked or deceitful in fathering his work. Envying no *eclât*, he coveted no contemporary fame, but lived on perfectly happy in having hope for the good his work would do in the future. If he held it better to let effort gain an end under a feigned name, to prevail over dull humanity or stolid will, there is nothing in the idea to condemn, but in the unselfish practice everything to admire and honour. The same design is the spirit of modern anonymity, exerting so potent influence in public discussion. When given up in yielding all to popular clamour a new and horrid tyranny will verify the forethought that warned against a time "when freedom will find in the printing office no security." The rigor of a censor invoked by a "free" press is a menace that will recoil on its own freedom. Every man in power being a coward—Cæsar himself quailed at the croaking of an Augur, till fear again filled him with trembling courage—every printing Pope or political potentate would coward-like gag that utterance which his own stupidity provokes. The Hydra-headed monster will one day cause the removal of the politic feint of hiding real names of genuine writers under feigned names in allegory; and these will again do what Bacon tells us had been done when a state incendiary called the King Julius, in respect of his empire, and the Queen Agrippina, to make "a play of both Court and Kingdom;" and in so doing let out his own secret.

How finely this mystic "imagination wrought upon the greatest men and matters" well appears in the epilogue to *Henry IV*. There it is said Sir John Falstaff is not meant for Sir John Oldcastle, for he died a martyr. The meaning of the retractation has hitherto baffled ingenuity; and yet it can be easily pointed to as a fact in Bacon's personal history. For an old *Monk-morality* play having long had Oldcastle, the resolute Puritan, familiar and odious as a dissolute comrade, as he really had in youth been, of young Prince Hal, the gross burlesque was unhappily copied into the first part of *Henry IV.* But when in 1594, the second part of that trilogy came to be written, the proper name of John Oldcastle was altered to John Falstaff, for "offence being worthily taken by personages descended from his title." The aggrieved individual was the captious Lord Cobham, whose duplicity brought Raleigh into a fatal scrape. Cobham was at the time of the play a colleague of Bacon in an inquiry into a conspiracy hatched to assassinate the Queen, and get rid of her and her sectaries; and the inheritor of Oldcastle's title felt sore at seeing the one thing he had to be proud of, the name of his great ancestor, unwittingly represented as "An aged counsellor to youthful sins." The complaint was made in the hearing of one ever ready to right a wrong, and the name in the play was altered accordingly. The man who made the change was at heart a Puritan. Lady Bacon's appeal to her cousin Burghley, adjuring him to relent and mitigate his colleague Whitgift's rigor on her chosen sect, showed her feeling toward the creed for which Oldcastle "died a martyr." Her son took his religion as he took his mind and feature from his mother, and knew with her that "the state of knowledge is ever a *Democratie*, and that prevaileth which is most agreeable to the senses and conceits of people."

By way of set-off to the legend and libel in *Henry IV.*, the biographical drama entitled *Sir John Oldcastle* represents the brave Lollard pleasingly to those who held him "in honourable memory." From the manner in which it was carried out, there can therefore remain very little doubt but that the alteration of the name of Oldcastle to that of Falstaff, like that from Corambis, in the original draft of *Hamlet*, to Polonius in the finished play, to personate Poley, Walsingham's favourite domestic spy, serves to trace the poet home.

This remarkable Oldcastle episode, and Hamlet's order to see the players well used, as they are "the abstract and brief chronicle of the time," "the purpose of playing, whose end, both at the first and now, was and is to hold as 'twere the mirror up to nature," accord with the Baconian definition of dramatic poetry as History made visible ; for plays are meant to be shown, not merely read, as Stephen Gosson argued. They appeal to vision.   Through the eye they educate, for,

> "The eye sees not itself
> But by reflection from some other thing."

The objective or visual mode of learning history is thus explained in the same manner in play and treatise.   The drama says :—

> "Since you know you cannot see yourself
> So well as by reflection, I your glass
> Will modestly discover to yourself
> That of yourself which you yet know not of."

And then the treatise likewise observes :—"For who can by often looking in the glass discern and judge so well of his own favour, as another with whom he converseth ?"

This agreement shows the drama may fairly be ascribed to one who felt himself able to benefit mankind, by a mind with "a kind of affinity for truth," and with all his thoughts bent on the glory of his country ; actuated as he was by an innate, not a simulated goodness, the drama was ancillary to his wider scheme ; and in this is found the key to the political purpose.   The reformer gains his end indirectly.   Admonition from an unknown hand will indicate faults and leave people "to find them out, rather as if it were by accident, than as prompted unto it."   This subtle lever to the stubborn heart is also applied in "admonition from a dead author, or a caveat from an impartial pen, whose aim neither was nor can be taken to be at any particular design, will prevail more, and take better impression than downright advice, which perhaps may be mistaken, as if it were spoken magisterially." Hence Gonzalo says—

> "I' the Commonwealth I would by contraries
> Execute all things."

And so would sapient Polonius

> "By indirections find directions out."

The indirect is likewise Bacon's method. He would effect reform on a plan wise folks ever act on when wanting good government. The blaring way will not evolve order out of anarchy. That is done by "work truly divine, which cometh *in aura leni* without noise or observation." In turbulent times public ills are never well treated by direct meddling; for, "in all human governments those who are at the helm can introduce what they desire for the good of the people more successfully by pretext and indirect ways than directly." In this way

> "The helms o' the state"

like knowing pilots guide their vessel.

The silent way of "the ignorant statesman" may be called cunning or Machiavellian, but extolled or reviled it agrees with what

> " We do learn
> By those who know the very nerve of the state,
> His givings out were of an infinite distance
> From his true meant design."

And the philosophic aphorism is spoken in dramatic phrase to which admirers may not so readily demur.

> " And that's not suddenly to be perform'd,
> But with advice and silent secrecy."

To emphasize the truth that rulers are slow to learn, Bacon adds :—" Nay, even in mere natural things you may deceive nature sooner than force her ; so inefficient and self-impeding are all things which are done directly ; whereas on the other hand the indirect and insinuating way proceeds smoothly and gains its end." The way of nature is winding and roundabout, and her manner is imitated in all the wiser kinds of human governments. In the same winding way the breaker of a natural law is eventually punished, and so is it shown to be in the great modern natural drama.

If great orators driving to political extremes knew the genius of the drama they would not dwell more on action than on reaction ; but " the empiric of Parliament, ever moved most by that he last had heard," like "a scurvy politician," never caught an inkling of "the divine science" from Plato; divine ethic from Æschylos; nor of that philosophical politic from Bacon and the renascence drama, that reared true greatness in Britain. From that drama a whole doctrine of conduct or rule of life can be framed identical with the ethic imbuing Baconian learning. The systems agree in moral sense, retributive justice, divine ordering in human life, intuitive sense of good and evil; principles taught in antithetic parable, and in an order directed with all the precision of a natural law. Both reveal one conscience, one piety, one obligation of right over might. In both, mind and brain are mated, male and female, to breed thought; and spiritual sorrows of the one are known to differ from corporeal diseases in the other. Like literary tastes give fruits of one culture, range of reading, and scope of reflection. Classical allusions of one form and quality are drawn direct from original works, often long before those written in strange tongues were turned into the vernacular. Indeed, so intimately uniform is the organic structure of the two systems of moral instruction that, in very technical phrase, one can be called *homologous* of the other; that is to say, both are contrived on a common plan, modified and adapted each for a special purpose; the two even often vying with each other in syntactic solecism or literary blunder. Mixing their metaphors in like ridiculous fashion, if one tremble to encounter "a sea of troubles," so does the other waive away "a sea of matter," or laud a king who "watered new dignities with the bounty of his lands." Both cite from memory, and without noting sources of mental food, imbibe, absorb, ruminate, and re-produce living thought in one ideation. The protoplasm of all knowledge is digested in their economy. Alike in grandeur of idea, they each have a trivial way of repeating a noble or a blurred metaphor. Both hold "the mind of man framed as a glass capable of the image of the universal world." So sib are they that people aver one learned things by instruction which the other knew by revelation, as if he were "somewhat supernatural and divine;" for in no other way can they account for their marvellous parallelism.

In neither treatise nor in drama is the *Bible* ever named; yet in both the Sacred Scriptures are very freely cited, in a manner evincing perfect familiarity with earlier and later versions. Although Bacon often quotes the Greek and Latin texts, he usually prefers translations in vogue when he was a child, chiefly the *Geneva*, printed the year he was born. The *Septuagint* and the *Vulgate* were well known to him; but the main influence of Wickliffe and Tindale is traceable in the marked archaic form of his peculiar syntax, an indelible impress of early training equally discernible in the uninflected language of the drama. Of any thousand running words written with the mind off guard, easy, natural, informal, free, eight-tenths are purely Saxon. The critique of Hume wherein the critic thought he found in both a "want of simplicity and purity of diction, with defective taste and elegance," is a tacit admission of their identity. But Hume's antagonism to the politic, philosophy, and religion, of treatise and drama, would tincture his opinion with a colouring from Voltaire, whose thought on Deity, Human Nature, and Moral Sentiment, differed from theirs, but agreed with his own perturbed notion. Nay, the very opinion that the poet was "ignorant of theatrical art and conduct" bears out the belief that the plays were not the work of a practical actor; and in so far Hume is right, for they were originally left undivided into acts or scenes, as if meant to be read, as they were read, in the beginning, in running dialogue, without shifting scenery other than what could be drawn by the hearer's imagination, when whisked from a bed-room to a battle-field, a palace to a prison, on the instant, with no help from daubery, or anything to see save the changes in the actor's visage. Therefore is Hume's animus against Philosopher and Dramatist alike an undesigned testimony that between them reigned one sovereign grace and majesty, to whom he owned no allegiance.

But although treatise and drama are equally full of aptly applied Scriptural allusions, there is in the two works a notable difference in the manner of using these illustrative passages. In the former the citations are always earnest, serious, and ratiocinative, as fitly becomes the graver argument they help to maintain; in the latter, in altering, modifying, or eliding to adapt the words to fit the individual characters employing them in dialogue, the poet often gives the sacred text a gibing, ironical, or sarcastic turn, with a levity rather grievous to misapprehending piety, as if the quaint jesting peculiar to the time at which he wrote were the poet's own profane scoffing, rather than faithful records of common talk and ordinary habit among thoughtless worldlings whose history he made visible. In modern *pseudo*-philosophic jargon, the blurred texts would be called *objective*, not *subjective* alterations. Whether the putative poet really had that full fervor in Scripture lore, or not, is quite unknown, apart from inference derivable from the drama itself, although it might well be urged that, as in the stirring times of his youthful years, the *Geneva Bible* was a very popular book in every Puritan home, there can be little doubt about his having often heard it read, or been even called upon to read it. But whether Mary Arden and her spouse were Calvinist or Catholic is doubted but not known. Regarding the vagrant son, a card and dice box and a Toledo blade are among the few relics left for pilgrims to worship at the shrine of him " whose grand object in life from his earliest days was," says Dyce, "the acquisition of a fortune to enable him to" reappear in the bravery of a fine town beau among rustic native townfolk, and leave wealth and a name for male children only to inherit. But along with the dubious signs of cards and fencing is never a hint of well-thumbed volume, to divert with graver thought the frivolous pastime.

On the other hand, Calvinistic Anne Cooke, wife to the "Fame and foundation of the English weal,"—he who took the legend "God, Loyalty, Freedom" for a watchword, a motto adopted by the "Son to the grave wise keeper, with a title more to the degree"—gave an example to her boy to make all Scripture in every version part of his polyglot erudition. Hence, the very titles of his earlier works tell how their *Interpretation of Nature* rested on a basis of learning *Divine and Humane;* and hence also the reason why they abound in Scriptural passages that are, as in the drama, mostly interwoven with the texture of the piece, and rarely if ever formally quoted. The wording of the *Proverb* heading this chapter varies in every version from Wickliffe onward, but in none is the meaning more neatly given or pressly put than in Bacon's form, the *Geneva* being nearest; while the added comment far excels in depth and clearness even that offered in the new commentary, wherein the native grandeur of the old layman's might well have been retained, to show how "as if, according to the innocent play of children, the Divine Majesty took delight to hide His works, to the end to have them found out;" and when found out to further find "that a little natural philosophy inclineth the mind to atheism, but a further proceeding bringeth the mind back to religion," as even Moses, "God's first pen," or "the book of Job, pregnant and swelling with natural philosophy," or even Solomon the King, who "by donative of God compiled a natural history of all verdure, from the cedar upon the mountain to the moss upon the wall," could not well have added more.

Indeed, so fully persuaded was Bacon that the silent way of Nature and Scripture was the true way to form an abiding creed in science and faith, and so keenly alive was he to the glaring errors in various versions used, and the odium thereby thrown through defects by nicknamers of the "breeches," the "treacle," and the "bug" or "bogie" *Bible* that blotted literature, hindered belief, and laid believers open to taunt from enemies at home and abroad for heretic differing where reform, if right, ought to be all after one platform, that, not silent in an argument he had travelled in before, yet holding aloof as "a man that standeth off, and somewhat removed from the plot of ground, doth better survey it and discover it than those which are upon it," "for lookers-on many times see more than gamesters, and the valley best discovers the hill," he did prevail upon the King to provide for his realm an uniform translation. Whether the idea were his, or a happy thought of Dr. Reynolds, there can be no doubt that the King adopted, and urged on the Bishops to adopt, the principal changes Bacon recommended. When the "careful selection of revisors, made by some unknown but very competent authority" were set to work "a set of rules was drawn up for their guidance, which has happily come down to modern times among the very few records that remain of this great undertaking. By whom they were framed is not known." But, whether sifted and passed through several hands or not, as is by Mr. Blunt guessed, these concise rules have a homogeneity, breadth, and vigour leaving no wonder how well the work was carried on in their spirit; they pointed the way as Bacon ever did; while they are undoubtedly allied to the *Observations on a Libel*, 1594, *On Church Controversies*, 1603, and other works of similar import written by Bacon about that time.

It may perhaps by some be thought over-straining a point to dwell so long on the analogy in question; but yet, if it be remembered that the increasingly popular work by Bishop Wordsworth, on the knowledge and use of the *Bible* shown in the *Drama*, urges the contrast with Bacon's more meagre knowledge as evinced in his writings, as a proof of the poet's superior attainments, the reader will no doubt form a very different opinion. Speaking of that inferiority the reverend author remarks that, "while most of the great laymen of that great Elizabethan age—Lord Bacon, &c.— have paid homage to Christianity, if not always in their practice, yet in the convictions of their understandings and in the profession of their faith, none of them has done this so fully or so effectually as Shakespeare." As this assertion by so good an authority might, by the nine out of ten who, as Macaulay observes, "talk of Bacon, but never read his works," be accepted and set against proof of the opposite here brought forward by a layman unlearned in Scripture, the latter to avail ought to be complete, and this finish can be given out of the reverend author's own pages, for therein it is said, " A British Churchman may be allowed to please himself in fancying Shakespeare as an occasional hearer of Bishop Andrewes—the greatest poet listening to the greatest preacher of the age; and had he been present when that admirable divine delivered his 'Exposition of the Seventh Commandment,' he could not have laid down the first principles more accurately than he has done in *Troilus and Cressida*, where Hector speaks respecting the duty of restoring Helen to her husband Menelaus."   Now, it surely can hardly be needful to remind Doctor Wordsworth that Bishop Andrewes was a friend of Bacon's student days, being then preacher at St. Giles's, and a man whom throughout his life he held in special reverence; the first to encourage him in his views, ever his literary inquisitor, and whose impressive sermons he often enough heard preached, leaving no doubt about his intimate acquaintance with their spirit and their doctrine.

This argument may be further strengthened by pointing out many words that are generally thought to be peculiar to the *Bible and* the *Drama,* but which equally belong to Bacon's works, as, for example, the word *bewray*, noted by Bishop Wordsworth as occurring in *Scripture and* in *Coriolanus;* but it is also found in Bacon's *Report* on Lopez, the traitor who " came too late to this shift, having first *bewrayed* his guilty conscience." A like use of other odd words in unusual meanings, as *aspersion* in the better sense, *perfite* for perfect, and more, might likewise be offered to illustrate even in minor details an all-pervading unity, leading to the belief that the Biblical lore in the treatise and that in the drama are one, thus showing the works to be somehow

" A little more than kin."

IV

THE PLAYS POLITICALLY GROUPED.

" They are the abstract and brief chronicles of the times."

" True history may be written in verse."

IN connecting the series of plays forming the body of dramatic poetry now named renascence drama with the politics that determined the fate of England as a Protestant state, they will be found to form two grand groups, an earlier and a later, the former marking the era of the elder Cecil; the latter the era of the equally potent Villiers, two chiefs modified by their times; one wisely plastic and yielding, the other tempered with fervent fortune. Each group is accordingly deeply ingrained with corresponding peculiarities. The particular plays of the earlier group are remarkable for being hopeful of the future, while many of the latter group, as *The Tempest, King Henry VIII.*, and *Timon of Athens*, are painful retrospects of political life. In Prospero, Wolsey, and Timon, a misanthrope reviews the causes that mar the patriot and sour philanthropy, the doleful quillets of the Clown in *Othello* marking it too of the later sort, that when the play is over leave on the mind sadness without a ray of hope.

The earlier group began while England reeled recovering political life after the terror reign of Mary Tudor, and ran on amid plots to release Mary Stuart, when captive "Queen of the Castle;" or else restore the Lady Arbella to her claimed right of a true heritor. Through the transition time Burghley administered the old, while gliding into the new, polity. The "sly old fox" cared little for forms of faith as long as he could rule the country; hence, the elder Bacon at his elbow had no hard work to jog him on to the *viâ media*, and still less trouble had the younger in guiding him along the way, though he had to dissemble carefully in working out his ideas for a reformed commonwealth. As one of his courses he had to devise parable and allegory framed on Greek lines, to effect reform; and to influence the mind of the

country he " put his patch upon the stage."   When
Bacon declared in debate that the King of Spain
had to be dealt with as a lion, and either tied or
tamed, and that in Scotland, France, and Spain,
England had three formidable enemies to cope
with, he spoke what is paraphrased in the play,
thus :—

> " But there's a saying very old and true :
>   ' If that you will France win,
>   Then with Scotland first begin.' "

Then, again, similar words and like sentiments
are repeated in play and state paper where it is
explained how persecution multiplies foes, " like
Hydra's heads—upon one cut off, seven grow
up :"—

> " And rebels' arms triumph in massacres !
>   They grow like Hydra's heads."

In the same speech, they who held that utility
and wealth are the springs of a trading and warlike
people, and called money the sinews of war, were
told that these means were better found in " the
very sinews of the arms of valiant men," that is,
in the words of the play :—

> " These are his substance, sinews, arms, and strength ; "

for thus did Talbot, in the play, and Bacon, in
the Senate, address the country on a threatened
invasion.   The drama was then no unmeaning

pageant, but as eloquent in war fervour as was the oration that roused the Commons to active patriotism. Not long after that time another state paper explained to the king how the true greatness of Britain would arise from an united kingdom that must assume an honourable part in the affairs of Europe; an union that when consummated would "make a new sun to rise in the west." In the same spirit the hero in the drama would endeavour to

> "Awake remembrance of those valiant deeds."

> "And if I live until I be a man,
> I'll win our ancient right in France again,
> Or die a soldier, as I liv'd a king."

For once in drama, English, Irish, Welsh, and Scots come together on the scene, to watch young Harry, sporting in valour, like a lion's cub that, unlike Spain, would neither be "tied nor tam'd."

Along with the military pageant to charm the ruder sort of people and through the popular theatre "on their imaginary forces work," were recondite analogies drawn from natural philosophy to engage the more intelligent. In courtly logic, it might even be of one "writing philosophy like a Lord Chancellor," as Harvey gibed, the studious King was taught how a "loadstone draws inferior to superior powers, as iron in atoms cleave to the magnet, but in mass will, like a true patriot, with appetite of amity, fall towards the centre of the earth;" or, in other words, gave a clear account of the law of gravitation, which was until then unheard of, save therein and in the drama, wherein it is equally plainly enounced in the same terms :—

> " But the strong base and building of my love
> Is as the very centre of the earth,
> Drawing all things to it."

Writing of the great service rendered to philosophy by Bacon in suggesting this attraction, this gravitation, which guides suns and planets in their orbits, and which directs an iron bar towards the centre of the earth, Voltaire remarks :—" But what sagacity in Bacon to have imagined what no one else had thought of!" But Voltaire forgot that the dramatist had also thought of the same law, and enounced it at the same time, in nearly identical terms !

Accompanying these kindred thoughts and words are allusions to the force that could

> " Control the moon, make flows and ebbs."
> " As well forbid the sea for to obey the moon."
> " Govern'd as the sea is by the moon."
> " The thick rotundity of the world."
> " Does the world go round ?"—

all apt in one repeating words about the pensile globe, while debating with Gilbert on magnetism, or with Galileo on tides, and arguing at length still open problems whether the earth were central or planetary, and did indeed go round. The owner of the only original portrait of Copernicus would in due time fitly urge Baranzano to work out with improved instruments the astronomical doubts with which the drama is so marvellously adorned. His clear idea of causation in conversion of force, in fire converting fuel to heat, as the living body converts food into life, gave vitality to the political drama while enunciating truths that science has only lately confirmed. In truth, poetry, science, philosophy, and policy contrived to combine four divided and often jarring kingdoms into one united compact power; gave England, as centre of the aggregate, her "proper place in the politics of Europe," and by "sober foresight" did so "lay the corner stone of the mightiest monarchy in Europe." The credit of the achievement is often claimed for Elizabeth, who, knowing better, candidly awards the merit and honour to her own "ignorant statesman," as the due of one ever telling the Commons what would "be true of the valour of a warlike nation, if we did hold ourselves worthy, either to recover our ancient rights, or to revenge our late wrongs, or to attain the honour of our ancestors, or to enlarge the patrimony of our posterity," exactly as the nation were fired to win their ancient rights again by the cognate fervid eloquence of the drama.

The group of English historical plays that appeared between 1591 and 1599 all relate to dynasty policy. Thus *King John*, now invariably viewed as a political play, not adhering to chronicle, but made up of parts of three different reigns to complete an allegory defending, exactly as Bacon defended, the Queen against efforts to depose her for a flaw in her birthright, is one of the finest arguments for England's independence, and one that can never be thoroughly understood nor fully appreciated until read in conjunction with Bacon and his political purpose. He, who after his father still adjured the Queen never to raise the question, ever

> " Wished the sleeping of this business ; never
> Desired it to be stirred ; but oft hinder'd "

all question from being brought up

> " Whether our daughter were legitimate."

By an ingenious inference the encomium on the Bastard extols her genealogy, making the

"I am I, howe'er I was begot,"

ring like her own defiant words ; for Queen Elizabeth, "of ever renowned memory," trusted, like Falconbridge, to personal merit no less than to lineage for her popularity in putting on

"The lineal state and glory of the land."

Under the prudent counsels of wise far-seeing patriots, whose end was vividly illumined by the light of the drama, the perilous era on which hung poised the fate of England as a free or a subject state was safely got over in favour of her entire freedom, autochthony, and perfect independence of Pope or of papal legate. But, to give still further warning how to act, the Queen and her pondering Ministers were also shown the terrific reign of Richard III. in allegory, picturing to them how the royal fiend, "though he were king in possession, and the rightful inheritors but infants, could never sleep quiet in his bed till they were made away," and further how by his defeat, after unnatural slaughter among brothers and fathers, and mothers and sisters and sons, and all sorts of kindred, the roses white and red were at length peacefully joined in one fair flower that Elizabeth inherited, and made to flourish, and so, by a parable plainly to be read, proved her menaced title good. And like that play, Bacon is never weary of dwelling on the way in which the Queen united in her nobility and in her beauty the roses white and red; nor of telling people how civil feuds are infinitely more cruel, fierce, and foolish than foreign warfare; and such were the cruel Wars of the Roses. Hence those plays wear all the intense sectarian feeling of the time at which they were written, mingled with Bacon's benign toleration; they are, as he is, full of respect for all sorts of royalty and clergy. Thus, when the Jesuit libeller would "round the Pope and the King of Spain in the ear by seeming to tell a tale to the people of England," Bacon's spirited and prompt reply at once freed "regal dignity from the recognition of a foreign superior." On no point is Bacon, and the drama, keener than when repelling foreign yoke; for they both fervently proclaim that a country subject to tribute cannot be great, prosperous, or free; and the way to subjugate England again is to make her a parish of the Papal See. This aphorism forms the refrain of these conventionally-styled historical dramas as of Bacon's political writings, speeches in Parliament, and court devices. In all he ever contends for sovereignty and liberty. That is the burden of his reply to the invective in Parson's *Responsio*, which attacks the Queen's Government as if it were degenerate by having cast off papal authority. The play is clearly a political allegory on the same subject of her position, title to the crown, and the unsettled succession. The dialogue in *King John* and Bacon's words might replace one another; for he speaks about the " instruments that are never failing about princes, which spy into their humours, and second them; yea, many times without their knowledge, pursue them further than themselves would," precisely as John complainingly says :—

> " It is the curse of kings to be attended
> By slaves that take their humour for a warrant
> To break within the bloody house of life,
> And on the winking of authority,
> To understand a law."

Not only are Bacon's words exactly the same as those in the play, but they were also written at the same time as the play, and on the same political question. Again, on the menaced intervention of Spain and Rome in England's affairs, Bacon says :—" But one thing I am persuaded of, that no king of Spain nor bishop of Rome shall umpire nor promote any beneficiary or feudatory king, as they designed to do even when the Scottish queen lived, whom they pretended to cherish. I will not retort the matter of succession upon Spain, but use that modesty and reverence that belongeth to the majesty of so great a king, though an enemy." This defiant yet withal deferential tone is equally maintained in the drama.

> " What earthly name to interrogatories
>   Can task the free breath of a sacred king?
>   Thou canst not, Cardinal, devise a name
>   So slight, unworthy, and ridiculous,
>   To charge me to an answer, as the Pope.
>   Tell him this tale ; and from the mouth of England
>   Add this much more,—That no Italian priest
>   Shall tithe or toll in our dominions ;
>   But as we, under Heaven, are supreme head,
>   So under Him, that great supremacy
>   Where we do reign, we will alone uphold,
>   Without th' assistance of a mortal hand."

Than these two declarations, the political and the allegorical, nothing could be nearer alike, for they are essentially one, and both were uttered in the same year. Alluding to lines in one of these kindred plays that are " instinct with glorious inspiration," Mr. Heraud avers that "such a passage might have been written by Bacon." But that eminent critic, though quoting the passage just cited from *King John*, does not compare it with the corresponding passage now added from Bacon, to note whether Bacon was not really author of both, for this comparison is now the only remaining critical deficiency. In speaking policy by "the mouth of England," the drama is as political as Bacon's state paper.

Among other defects of the drama, objected to by Hume, the great historian declares the plays to show in the poet no sympathy for civil liberty; in reply to which the aim of *King John* may be adduced in refutation; for, while the dramatist had no feeling for empirics or strouting politicians of Jack Cade's school, he yet evinces the warmest sympathy for every effort to elevate England to a free power, by throwing off the shackle, to let her take the first step towards constitutional liberty, precisely as Bacon aimed.

Naming Cade will recall the political play of *Henry VI.*, whoever wrote or altered that *Yorke and Lancaster* or White Rose and Red Rose trilogy. True to history, Cade stands typical of every political mountebank in any age who vows reformation to do away with rule by law for reft by administration, promising a big loaf and free wine-pump at the state's score for duped louts in clouted shoon, and threatening broken heads and flaming homes for silken-coated slaves their oppressors.   For did not Jack, in order when most out of order, bid the gulled people strike heads, burn bridges, break open gaols, hang all who could read or write, and make maids and wives as free as heart could wish or tongue can tell ?   And what more could be got from a Liberal ?

> " Away ! burn all the records of the realm ;
> My mouth shall be the only Parliament,"

is alike the will of ruthless king and merciless plebeian.

In *Cymbeline* the purpose of aiding the Crown to free itself from the thrall of Rome is very evident.   Although this drama is not classed along with the group conventionally styled Historical, it nevertheless is as accurately so as any of the number.   The allegory reveals how England of old stoutly refused to pay tribute to Rome, in the time of Cæsar, and therefore to refuse again would maintain " The natural bravery of our isle." "Why tribute? Why should we pay tribute?" Because, says Bacon, "A people that pay tribute are not fitted for empire," and he wanted to rear in England "the mightiest monarchy in Europe." He would not even succumb to Cæsar, grandly as he thought of him. And, by the way, his idea of Cæsar is expressed in almost the same glowing panegyric, as that

> "Julius Cæsar—whose remembrance yet
> Lives in men's eyes, and will to ears and tongues
> Be theme and hearing ever."

> "There be many Cæsars
> Ere such another Julius."

> "Cæsar's ambition,—
> Which swell'd so much, that it did almost stretch
> The sides o' the world."

This is the Cæsar of whom Bacon often writes in the most exalted strain of eulogy, as for example, "Cæsar, his ambition reserved, the finest spirit of the world;" and so on of many other expressions, as will be seen in the remarks on the drama under his name.

One portion of the *Cymbeline* trilogy is derived from an Italian novel which was not translated at the time the play is supposed to have been written, which, though it be a difficulty to commenters, is none to those who admit the Baconian authorship. The name and character of Imogen was thence derived, although she is made a thoroughly English woman ; while the frequent naming of Britain, "the sea-girt isle," and her threatening invaders, entirely agree with Bacon's efforts to name the kingdom anew, and prepare for union. His labours in this direction began before James came to the throne, and were common to himself and to his brother " though by design (as between brethren) dissembled," their duration being coincident with the computed period of the drama.

In the *King Lear* is another half historical, wholly political, drama, the leading object of which is evidently to warn some royal personage of the peril involved in abdicating in favour of some trusted one who might in the covetousness and frailty of human nature possibly prove ungrateful. The warning against such a disposal of the crown is clearly enough conveyed in the words :—

> " How, in one house,
> Should many people, under two commands,
> Hold amity ? "

The evil or danger of naming a successor which was ever present to Elizabeth's mind, to such a degree that every one about her was forbidden under dire penalty to even remotely allude to it, is also foreshadowed, or thinly veiled, under the wrapping up which cannot conceal the personality of one who was

> " Every inch a Queen."

Love and anger

> " Mov'd her
> Not to a rage : patience and sorrow strove
> Who should express her godliest. You have seen
> Sunshine and rain at once : her smiles and tears
> Were like a better day,"—

or a woman whose passion flitted every instant, but who could command feeling, and subdue it under the control of public duty, and who in that wonderful restraint or self-control found one secret of her singular power over those with whom she came into contact. Ever "whistling for the ablest men" to her councils, she better than Goneril knew who were "worth the whistle." Of the sources of the main and subordinate plots in the *Lear* trilogy commenters have long had doubts, and no two agree about the date of the play, or its relation to a former play of the same title. The inquiry is now given over in despair, the very latest editor saying, " For me it is sufficient that we have the play." In this avowal Mr. Furness adds of the plays themselves that when he is lost in their grandeur and their beauties he is "indifferent as to when they were written, where they were written, or even by whom they were written"—"they stand by themselves, written by no mortal hand;" the poet "has faded, and left not a wrack behind,"—a rhapsody full of as rank ingratitude as is the crime of Goneril or Regan, and worthier the raving of some literary epicure or meanly selfish book-glutton than of a refined and elegant compiler, who, if he could clearly discern the real poet through his works, would enjoy the one and honour the other all the more. When the great purpose of the plays is sublimed away, leaving only a distillment for literary luxury, they will soon pall upon the appetite.

As for the political purpose of *Lear* looming through its captivating grandeur, the peculiar treatment given to the word "Britain" is perfectly significant; for the change from "Englishman" to "Britishman" denotes, it is argued, the date of composition to be about the time of the union; and no doubt the fact allies the play to *Cymbeline*, as already mentioned.

Thus, then, was the political purpose of the renascence drama gained. The Queen was influenced unawares by these ancient pieces making her own precarious case visible, in which she " saw her way laid down as in a map." After beholding herself in them as in a mirror, she would neither name a successor, admit bastardy, abdicate, nor be deposed; and if Edmund the base is ironical over the "fine word legitimate," and brawls

" Now, gods, stand up for bastards !"

yet Falconbridge, the brave, is on the same theme in earnest.

Torturing political offenders in the Tower is, in these dramas, drawn in harrowing detail. When men beheld the horrible reflection in the theatre the brutal work was stopped. Once Bacon *officially* witnessed the revolting scene, and made the horror of gouging eyes go beyond the inhuman. Ferocity alone could shock the truculence of the time on senseless barbarity. In the social reform of that mode of inflicting corporal punishment is another example of the salutary influence of the renascence drama.

To the foregoing examples, taken from the grander works and plays dealing with greater problems of international polity, may be added some illustrations from minor politics, touching the more homely matters of usury, or duelling, excess or abuse of which required a lash from the dramatist or a law from the legislature. In *The Merchant of Venice*, the one, and in *Romeo and Juliet*, the other vice is assailed. If Bacon had a hand in the composition of either play, it ought to show itself through corresponding incidents narrated in his avowed writings, wherein he deals with similar subjects, and this will be found the case. Thus, *The Merchant of Venice* was printed in the summer cf 1598, about the time when a "Lombard, noted much for extremities and stoutness upon his purse," having Bacon held "in bond for £300 principal," and "handling it as upon despite," like a veritable Shylock, "urged it to have had me in prison." These singular phrases again appear in the wording of a draft in Bacon's handwriting, of date or occasion unknown, for a law to put down usury. This draft sets out in a dramatic preamble that many are by usury undone and overthrown. "When men are in necessity, and desire to borrow money, they are answered that money cannot be had, but that they may have commodities."

Continuing the same strain, Shylock adds :—

> " I cannot instantly raise up the gross.
> What of that?
> A wealthy Hebrew of my tribe
> Will furnish me."

The preamble further sets out how the obligation of a loan had to be got, if at all, at "extreme high rates," the borrower to be "wrapt in bonds and counter-bonds," and be "subject to penalties and suits of great value." It also ordained that usury should be punished by heavy fine, imprisonment, and pillory.

Almost a year before the date of the play, it happened that Bacon had got among the Lombards—" pardon me if I name them by the street they live in"—and had to humbly "desire the help of two so good friends " against the "slipping and incertain or cunning dealing" of one "standing to be redeemed," in a manner perfectly dramatic. The usurer did, when "standing to be redeemed in so instant a quantity of time, plunge me to seek money or to forfeit my land ;" while the gloating exactor kept sneering at the "collateral pawn" of friends who "neither lend nor borrow upon advantage;" nor "merchandizing in a contract, each looking to advantage."

Private wrong thus incited Bacon to take public action against usury; and hence date and diction in draft and drama agree.

When Bacon threw the scandal of his arrest by the sergeant, who came

> " And clapt him on the back ;
> And laid him into prison strong,
> And sued his bond withal,"

into dramatic form, he but adapted two popular tales that left him as a play-writer little to invent in composing the tragi-comedy.   In both tales money is described :—

> " Or like a filthy heap of muck,
> That lieth in a hoard ;
> Which never can do any good,
> Till it be spread abroad ;"

" A mass of wealth no better than a heap of muck, to be spread to many useful purposes."

It strains no analogy to compare the pun on the plea of the culprit Hogg, who claimed kin to Bacon, that "hog was not Bacon till hung," with the verse,

> " His life was like a barrow hogge,
>   That liveth many a day,
>   Yet never once doth any good,
>   Until men will him slay."

And when the Jew will not dine "to smell pork," yet will "buy with you, sell with you, talk with you, walk with you, and *so following*," the tail "and so following" winds up a truly Baconian category.

In the theatre the modern readers of the play begin to feel the indirect or philosophic motive of the drama, and trust to the intelligent, rather than appeal to the uneducated, portion of the audience. Actors have faith in the higher forms of their fine art, and are not now afraid of poetry on the stage. Thus lately wrote a critic on a great living player who has been enlightening his patrons on the character of Shylock, and has quickened attention to the meaning of the poet in its delineation. The lesson read in it is toleration, not rudely blurted out, so as to be offensive to the prejudices of the age, but artfully to commend it by adroitly treating it in the roundabout winding way that Bacon counsels, and as a master of persuasion succeeded in his mission. To the critic the actor well depicts the various moods of Shylock's disturbed mind, and in all redeems it from the vulgar elements that once entered so largely into the popular idea. "That mistake is now annihilated for ever." It is therefore possible to conquer popular prejudice regarding the true meaning of the renascence drama. From the advent of Irving it is already altered. The clouds chasing black shadows on the poet's drift rapidly clear away.

"The clouds as chariots swiftly scour the sky,"

leaving it clear and deeply

"All set with spangs of glittering stars untold,"

showing where the character of Portia has a "decidedly comic side, with a serious, almost tragic phase." Yet Portia is no abstraction of embodied wisdom. The play is a tragi-comedy to reform a great and growing evil of the time, acting on the Baconian theory of the true uses of dramatic poetry, and therefore agreeably to good sound common sense.

And if the author of that theory could touch off to the life, in a few neat, apt words, the traits of an exacting usurer, and the social evil of avarice, so could he delineate the finer·lines in Portia, as freely as he could Macbeth's psychology. To form the play, there was little to contrive in name or plot, these being ready to hand in earlier works. That Bacon had the learning indicated in the classical allusions peculiar to the play is well known. That he had feeling for the finer touches in the comedy, enough to make a hard lesson attractive by contrasting harsh usury with a purely æsthetic life, may be inferred from comparing the colloquy between Lorenzo and Jessica, on the effect of music on the affections of the mind, with Bacon's remarks on the same influence. Thus he similarly explains how quavering will please by agreeing with the glittering of light, as the moonbeams playing upon a wave; and how falling from a discord to a concord is sweetness in music by agreeing with the affections, which recover tone better after dislikes, as taste that is soon glutted with what is sweet alone. Thus the kinds of music operate upon the manners; and tunes and airs in their own nature have in themselves an affinity with the affections, and feed that disposition of the

spirits which they find, exactly as Jessica feels
and confesses to in saying,

"I'm never merry when I hear sweet music;"

and exactly as Lorenzo expatiates upon in very
Baconian style, telling her how for that

"The reason is, your spirits are attentive."

Music for the time will alter nature. To him
that hath not music in himself, nor is not moved
by concord of sweet sounds, the motions of his
spirits are dull as night, and dark as Erebus are
his affections. Either, therefore, the philosopher
here explains the poet, or the poet dramatizes
the philosopher. That the greater probability is
that both were one would now more forcibly than
ever appear from recent discussions on the source
of the plot and purpose of the play, in which
Mr. Spedding states that the purpose was precisely
in accord with Bacon's aim, while the plot was
derived from *Il Pecorone*, Italian tales not translated
into English before 1755, that the poet "had
either read or heard" of; and that "the changes
which he introduced were only such as the
conversion of a narrative into an actable play

required." To do this he must have been perfectly familiar with the Italian language, which was one of Bacon's accomplishments. If those disputants who are now entering so keenly into this controversy will include the papers and letters now for the first time associated with the play, they will soon find it necessary to give their discussion quite a new departure, that must bring them round to the true aim and authorship of the drama; and this they will the better do if they discard all trite and trivial test of variable verbiage, and try rather by parallels running along the lines of abstract thought and philosophic purpose that an inceptive mind will neither imitate nor alter, but keep the oneness ever quite apparent.

V

ROMEO AND JULIET.

" Civil brawls bred of an airy word."

" Dejected with a word or trivial disgrace."

THE passion picture of *Romeo and Juliet* is æsthetically viewed through the central figures, to whom the word-painting of the poet gives prominence and lustre. But the moral, for social and civic reform, is found in the filling in of the finely-touched background ; for the fate of the hero and heroine is only the effect of a habit rankling at the core of civic life, and a custom of privately righting private wrong, spreading from individuals to families, and thence to the whole body politic, which Bacon strove to abrogate and forbid, by showing the evil results as revealed in the dramatic allegory.

Usurpers, lynchers, vigilants, spies, secret judges, caucuses, strike at degrees in authority on which all settled forms of good government depend for their stability. Though " degrees, estates, and offices are oft deriv'd corruptly," yet—

" Take but degree away, and hark what follows ! "

" Then everything includes itself in power,
  Power into will, will into appetite ;
  And appetite, an universal wolf,
  So doubly seconded with will and power,
  Must make perforce an universal prey,
  And last eat up himself.
  Thus chaos, when degree is suffocate,
  Follows the choking."

The politics of the renascence drama uphold authority, venerate its very image, and tell why "a dog 's obey'd in office." The moral of authority is thus set forth in a paper on *Duels :*—

" When revenge is once extorted out of the magistrate's hand, contrary to God's ordinance, and every man shall bear the sword, not to defend, but to assail, and private men begin once to presume to give law to themselves, and to right their own wrongs, no man can foresee the dangers and inconveniences that may arise and multiply therefrom, from individuals to families and national quarrels, ending in anarchy and convulsion."

This was the gist of the first paper written by Bacon on taking office. He took the earliest opportunity to grapple with a great and growing evil. It was his first social reform in his public capacity. For years the idea of it had been working in his mind, and he seized the fit instant to inhibit the instinct ruling in half civilized society. As Escalus deplores the " civil brawls bred of an airy word," so Bacon regrets that any be " dejected with a word or trifling disgrace." He, more than any man, felt faction feuds between Essex and Cecil, feuds not unlike those between the houses of Montagu and Capulet. Loyal to Queen and country, Bacon, in trying to reconcile conflicting clans, offended both.

The politics of the time were therefore illustrated in two dramatic allegories—in *Romeo and Juliet*, a tragedy, and in *Troilus and Cressida*, a comedy, paired on the dual principle of the renascence drama, both framed to the life, telling how

" Ancient grudge breaks to new mutiny,"

and by private persons righting their own wrongs, according to "that other law of reputation," "giving the law an affront," exactly as Bacon taught. He, like the dramatist, contemned the dogma that might is right, upholding axiomatic morality and degree's priority,

" Which is the ladder to all high designs."

What Ulysses says about *Force* and *Right*,

"Between whose endless jar justice resides,"

is either paraphrased by the poet, or reiterated by the political dramatist, in Bacon's address to King James on *Duelling*. Indeed, so closely identifiable, in word, phrase, and sentiment, are the dialogues in the drama with the corresponding writings of the statesman, that they even emulate each other in perpetrating that remarkable literary blunder already referred to about young men and Aristotle's moral and political philosophy. The parallel does not diverge even at palpable mistake.

It should also be here remarked that in what the drama says through the mouth of Ulysses about

"The heavens themselves, the planets, and this centre,"

the words "*this centre*" refer to the earth, as centre of the universe, or planetary system at least; and, further, that the line

"And therefore is the glorious planet Sol"

makes the sun a subordinate planet; both allusions being in perfect accord with what Bacon was

then, at the date of *Troilus and Cressida,* alone
in England discoursing upon in regard to the
sidereal heavens, their ether and their inter-
attractions, and in a manner commanding Voltaire's
admiration, as of every thinker, no matter what
estimate he formed of Bacon's relation to poetry,
science, ethics, philosophy, or religion. What he
then wrote, and what was then written in the
drama, are the same; to both, the one idea
being alone confided; and, as Voltaire has indeed
admirably set forth, Bacon and the *Drama* were
at once together, on the *Globe Intellectual,*

"As iron to adamant, as earth to centre."

VI

THE SONNETS.

" I had, though I profess not to be a poet, prepared a sonnet."

" Who will believe my verse in time to come?"

THE political drift of *The Sonnets* is very plain. Printed in 1609, from manuscripts taken to the printer by some one who was not their author, the date of their composition is unknown. They are usually held to be the sonnets referred to by Meres, in the line in the *Wit's Treasury*, where the soul of Ovid is said to live in the " mellifluous and honey-tongued" poet, as " witness his *Venus and Adonis*, his *Lucrece*, his sugred sonnets among his private friends." This work by Meres was printed in 1598, eleven years before *The Sonnets* were in print. This is the only contemporary reference to sonnets written by the poet ; but whether the allusion be to the sonnets that are now extant, or not, is all conjecture. Far more probable is it that Francis Meres knew of sonnets handed about in manuscript among a circle of private friends, between 1594 and 1598, and which were printed in the latter year under the title of *The Passionate Pilgrim*. These verses are all highly amatory, and far more fitly described as "sugred" than the querulous, upbraiding, sour, and apologetic stanzas of the so-called sonnets that can only be called honeyed by misnomer. To prurient thought their half-concealing, half-revealing might convey fit suggestion, though they in tone be pure, chaste, amiable, and even solemn, some indeed acrid, compared with the loving songs in *Love's Labour 's Lost* and *The Pilgrim*. In this innuendo will be found the true criterion of their political meaning and of their real authorship ; for it will now be shown that the *Sonnet* written by Bacon, in 1600, for a friend to read to the Queen, and thereby win back her regard for her offending truant Essex, when the "lord of my love" lay under his last eclipse, is the composition known to literature as *The Sonnets*. In June, 1598, Essex behaved rudely, and provoked the Queen to give him a box on the ear that made him lay his hand on the hilt of his sword, mutter some defiant words, and leave the room in high dudgeon; but they were soon afterwards reconciled, and he went to Ireland, but quickly returned with the fatal Tyrone memorial. Rightly or wrongly, this action was called treason, or misprision, and Essex was ordered to keep within his own house until the affair was considered in Council. Meanwhile Bacon tried by every means in his power to mollify the anger of the Queen, and prevail on Essex to conciliate her wrath, pleading on him to confess, and not justify his conduct, as his best policy. In the famed *Apology*, written in 1603, to vindicate himself from " mad slanders by mad ears believed," and from the " libel successor to legend " in " a tale shaped in London forge," he states what is either true or false, that after vainly entreating his friend, the chivalrous Earl, to shun arms as unfit for one of his temperament and opportunity as prime favourite, when foreseen sorrow came, he " with honest heart did occupy the utmost of my wits and adventure my fortune to reintegrate my friend's." This part of intercessor he fulfilled " by earnestness of speech, by writing, and by all

the means I could devise," trying to "pull him out of the fire;" appealing to the better part of an angered woman touched on the tender side of sovereign authority by an ingrate, to "move her to yet turn the light of her favour towards" her erring hero. Relating all he did and tried to do on behalf of the wayward Earl, Bacon writes:—
"It happened a little before that time that her Majesty had a purpose to dine at Twickenham Park, at which time I had (though I profess not to be a poet) prepared a sonnet directly tending and alluding to draw on her Majesty's reconcilement to my lord, which I remember also I showed to a great person, and one of my lord's nearest friends, who commended it. This, though it be (as I said) but a toy, yet it showed plainly in what spirit I proceeded." This sonnet has never been found amongst Bacon's papers, nor has it ever been identified in print; in truth, no conjecture has hitherto been offered, as far as the writer is aware, of the probable fate of that missing sonnet. That Bacon's and *the Sonnets* were one is inferred from internal evidence almost to a literal certainty; a comparison of the phraseology, tropes, and metaphors in Bacon's letters, speeches, and papers

relating to the fatal episode in Essex's career with those in the poem, leaving no room for doubt. In a speech at the trial Bacon said :—" For you, my lord, should know that though princes give their subjects cause of discontent, though they take away the honours they have heaped upon them, though they bring them to a lower estate than they raised them from, yet ought they not to forget their allegiance." Now, the twenty-fifth stanza likewise pointedly alludes to a fallen favourite who till lately could

> "Of public honour and proud title boast."

Then follows direct reference :—

> " Great princes' favourites their fair leaves spread,
>   But as the marigold at the sun's eye ;
>   And in themselves their pride lies burièd,
>   For at a frown they in their glory die.
>   The painful warrior famousèd for fight,
>   After a thousand victories, once foiled,
>   Is from the book of honour razèd quite,
>   And all the rest forgot for which he toil'd.
>   Then happy I, that love and am belov'd,
>   Where I may not remove nor be remov'd."

Up till June, 1598, Essex had been the great princes' favourite, "famousèd for fight," but then came he under a frown that made that glory die ; while Bacon, holding no high office, could not be removed. But he, "still awake and true to his grounds, which he thought surest for his lord's good," said to this effect :—

"Madam, I know not the particulars of estate, and I know this that princes' actions must have no abrupt periods or conclusions, but otherwise I would think that if you had my Lord of Essex here with a white staff in his hand, as my Lord of Leicester had, and continued him still about you for society to yourself, and for honour and ornament to your attendance and Court in the eyes of your people, and in the eyes of foreign ambassadors, then were he in his right element." Thus did Bacon earnestly speak and write,

"To witness duty, not to show my wit,"

towards his hapless friend Essex, the

"Lord of my love,
When in disgrace with fortune and men's eyes."

And thus throughout the appealing song similies again and again recur that appear in the *Apology* and allied writings. In one the author calls himself no poet—"I do not profess to be a poet;" in the other, the poet invokes his "pupil pen" for a "lovely argument" that

"Deserves the travail of a worthier pen"

than what indites "these poor rude lines" in "the barren tender of a poet's debt;" and a more "polish'd form of well refinèd pen."

In connection with all these disclaimers of poetic verve, Bacon too professed not to be a poet, and was ever ready to exclaim,

" When shall you see me write a thing in rhyme?"

When the *Sonnets* were thought addressed to Elizabeth, their amatory tone forbade the idea of wooing songs from a youth to a woman who for her years might be his grandmother. The direct reading is indeed grotesque ; but as allegory there is no incongruity, and this is as they should be read.   Icarus's fortune had befallen Essex, who would fly with waxen wings, and when they broke, and left him toppling from the giddy heights of rebellion to the scaffold, among the devices to avert the fate were two feigned letters by Bacon, and the preparation of a sonnet.

The effort in the *Apology* to condone a "contempt," or treason, nearly brought the ardent pleader himself to the brink of a " misprision."

" And so my patent back again is swerving,
Thyself thou gav'st.
To thy great gift upon misprision growing,
Comes home again."

When the poet in the *Sonnets* sings,

"Whilst I, my Sovereign, watch the clock for you,"

Bacon's office of "watch-candle to my Sovereign" is at once suggested, as if it sung of one ever ready

"To play the watchman ever for thy sake;
For thee watch I."

So, likewise, when the *Sonnets* say—

"For canker vice the sweetest buds doth love,"

there "never was bud so fair but it might nourish a canker-worm" immediately occurs to memory, which might be filled with more agreeing metaphors than are required for an argument by analogy.

The identity of the certain great person to whom Bacon showed his sonnet, to show it again to the Queen, has an important bearing upon the authorship of the *Sonnets*. That it would be some favoured functionary of the royal household, a chamberlain, or page, or lord-in-waiting, is clear, for Elizabeth would not go to dine even with Bacon without some parade of state. If the accompanying great person were the young Earl Pembroke, or rather the then Lord Herbert, the mystery of dedication to "W. H." is solved. To William Herbert would be given *MSS.* of Bacon's sonnet, and he was the very man to read them privately among the friends of the putative author of the *Sonnets.* This is the more probable since it is admitted that their *MSS.* were given to the printer by some one who was not their author, and a "W. H." is "the only begetter" or obtainer for the printer.

Young Herbert had then been only three years in London, and as son of "Sidney's sister" had immediate entry into Court and literary circles. He was quickly taken with sonneteering, and when shown a poetical effusion by Bacon he would naturally aspire to rank with wits and poets by carrying it to the printer, and invite or have offered the complimentary dedication. That a name should be used to print under, even for private circulation among friends, was only complying with the censor's requirement, while a borrowed name would equally be required to cover the real author. But why should Bacon "prepare a sonnet directly tending and alluding to draw on her Majesty's reconcilement to my lord," rather than appeal direct to her sympathy? Bacon himself supplies the answer :—"As sometimes it cometh to pass that men's inclinations are opened more in a toy than in a serious matter."   "The Ætolians, in their talk, did more respect those which did overhear them than those to whom they directed their speech."   "In dealing with cautelous persons, whose speech is ever at a distance with their meanings, a man is not to regard what they affirm or what hold, but what they would convey under their pretended discourse, and what turn they would serve."   By applying the Ætolian oblique speech to the *Sonnets* their meaning becomes clear, without ambiguity.

In the opening stanzas a comely boy such as Pembroke then was, fresh from a country life, is adjured to wed, and perpetuate graces adorning mind and body in " this fair child of mine," before forty winters shall besiege his brow.   This beautiful youth, whom no fair damsel would disdain, was " now the world's fresh ornament," precisely as was then young Herbert, of whom all declared,

> " Thou art thy mother's glass, and she in thee
> Calls back the lovely April of her prime."

And he was enjoined not to

> " Die single, and thine image dies with thee,"

or be like the Maiden Queen, whom Bacon often gently chides because

> "A mate of fortune she would never take."

Painting the "lovely boy" Herbert, the poet sings :—

> "A woman's face, with Nature's own hand painted,
> Hast thou, the master-mistress of my passion.
> A woman's gentle heart, but not acquainted
> With shifting change, as is false woman's fashion ;
> An eye more bright than theirs, less false in rolling,
> Gilding the object whereupon it gazeth ;
> A man in hue all hues in his controlling,
> Which steals men's eyes, and woman's soul amazeth."

On the same chord is the song in praise of the Queen—"What life, what edge is there in those words and glances wherewith at pleasure she can give a man long to think, be it that she means to daunt him, to encourage him, or to amaze him ?"

Having drawn the portrait of young Herbert to the life—

> "Mine eyes have drawn thy shape, and thine for me
> Are windows to my breast "—

when, "her Majesty not liking to make windows into men's hearts and secret thoughts," the poet proceeds with the special object of the *Sonnets*. After pleading that

> "Th' offender's sorrow lends but weak relief,"

and also further complaining that

> " Thy adverse party is thy advocate,—
> And 'gainst myself a lawful plea commence :
> Such civil war is in my love and hate,"

the poet, like the pleader, then says :—

> " Two loves I have of comfort and despair,
> Which like two spirits do suggest me still :
> The better angel is a man right fair,
> The worser spirit a woman colour'd ill."

Next to duty and honour to the Queen, Bacon vows he best loves Essex. Yet, in 1600, between meddling with their lover-like tiffs, and drawing him out of the fire, or from under clouds and eclipses, adding to the letters he wrote for Essex hints about his own ill fortune, the better to feign the correspondence genuine, he falls out of favour with both, precisely as with the two loves of comfort and despair in the wailing sonnets ; for he said,—" Madam, I see you withdraw your favour from me, and now that I have lost many friends for your sake, I shall leese you too." " A great many love me not, because they think I have been against my Lord of Essex ; and you love me not, because you know I have been for him :" "yet will I never repent me, that I have dealt in simplicity of heart towards you both," precisely as with the two loves of comfort and despair in the *Sonnets.* In them, too, the word "*leese*" occurs once for the only time in the whole range of the poetical or dramatic writings; and it also occurs in the *Apology.*

The lines beginning with—

"No longer mourn for me when I am dead,
Than you shall hear the surly sullen bell,"

to excite pity, and anticipate remorse for hasty decision, when the offending Earl was confined to York House, in imminent peril of having a surly sullen bell toll after he had fled "from this vile world," unless the sonnet writer moved him to expiate his crime, or the angry Queen would reintegrate him, have their counterpart in the portion of the letter hinting at his lordship's "good and wise friends" who "do not only toll the bell, but even ring out peals, as if your fortune were dead and buried," without a possible restoring to favour.

The eighty-fourth verse flatters the assertive Tudor spirit in

"This rich praise—that you alone are you."

You alone are you! "I am I;" or, as the imperious Henry, emphasizing like his daughter, asks, "Who am I, ha?"

The lines on "lingering out a purposed overthrow," with a metaphor on a seditious noble in a decaying lily,

> "For sweetest things turn sourest by their deeds;
> Lilies that fester smell far worse than weeds,"

merely repeat Bacon's metaphor on the rebel noble, "for lilies that fester are more offensive than when weeds decay." The lines appeared in *Edward III.*, a doubtful play; and it is one of many repeated metaphors.

Equally remarkable are the words referring to the best mode of influencing the Queen, when compared in letter and sonnet. In dealing with Essex's case, Bacon found "the only course to be held with the Queen was by obsequiousness and observance:"

> "No, let me be obsequious in thy heart,
> And take thou my oblation, poor but free."

The wild talk in town about

> "Mad slanders by mad ears believèd be"

refers to the "tale shaped in London's forge" against Bacon, after the Queen's expressed suspicion that Bacon could not forget his old love for his friend to serve her cause fully, and led to a popular invention that he betrayed Essex. But, in a clear conscience he exclaims,

> "Prison my heart in thy steel bosom's ward,
>   But then my friend's heart let my poor heart bail."

In other words: Do with me what you will, but let me be my friend's bail,—very much in the form of Bacon's appeal for

> "One of her feather'd creatures broke away,"

he who was "to grow up feathers, especially ostrich's, or any other save of a bird of prey," and, "no man shall be more glad."

The peroration reads :—A thrall came to an offended mistress persuading her to cure her favourite's moral ailing, she thinking herself a great physician in all things. The thrall's own love fired her, yet her coolness was not overcome. The reading is true to History. Familiarity with the relations between Essex, Bacon, Herbert, and the Queen, makes obscure allusions plain. The reading needs no forced analogy, for Bacon himself gives the key to interpret his own parable.

In pleading for his friend Bacon metaphorically alluded to a fellow who undertook to cure gout, and made patients better at first, but left them worse, when the Queen said :—" I will tell you,

Bacon, the error of it: the manner of these physicians, and especially these empirics, is to continue one kind of medicine, which at the first is proper, being to draw out the ill humour, but after, they have not the discretion to change their medicine, but apply still drawing medicines, when they should rather intend to cure and corroborate the part." Then Bacon replied :—
" Good lord, Madam, how wisely and aptly can you speak and discerne of physic ministered to the body, and consider not that there is the like occasion of physic ministered to the mind; as now in the case of my Lord of Essex, your princely word ever was that you intended ever to reform his mind, and not ruin his fortune: I know well you cannot but think that you have drawn the humour sufficiently, and therefore it were more than time, and it were but for doubt of mortifying or exulcerating, that you did apply and minister strength and comfort unto him : for these same gradations of yours are fitter to corrupt than correct any mind of greatness."

Now, whether this may be deemed flat, or lively dialogue in prose : and one would hardly expect to hear blank verse employed in ordinary conversation on such an occasion: yet it is unquestionably a paraphrase of the pleading in the following lines in the *Sonnets* :—

> " My love is as a fever, longing still
>   For that which longer nurseth the disease ;
>   Feeding on that which doth preserve the ill,
>   Th' uncertain-sickly appetite to please.
>   My reason, the physician to my love,
>   Angry that his prescriptions are not kept,
>   Hath left me, and I desperate now approve
>   Desire is death, which physic did except.
>   Past cure I am, now reason is past cure,
>   And frantic-mad with evermore unrest ;
>   My thoughts and my discourse as madmen's are
>   At random from the truth vainly express'd."

Like her father, Elizabeth took pride in her skill in physic ; hence the subtlety of the refined flattery. An amateur physician, Bacon, like Lord Cerimon, knew the delight of studying the natural history of disease and cure, and the futility of trying to administer physic to the mind disordered,

> " As testy sick men, when their deaths be near,
>   No news but health from their physicians know."

The devil's tempers are ever worse to deal with than are God's diseases, and Bacon " commended mercy in her Majesty."

> " But when she saw my woful state,
>   Straight in her heart did mercy come,
>   Chiding that tongue that ever sweet
>   Was used in giving gentle doom."

The paradox on "*Time is*, and then *Time was*, and *Time would never be*," is referred to in the *Apology* as it appears in the *Sonnets*.

The more enduring monuments of learning compared with the fleeting work of power was already noted as a theme with Bacon, and may again be taken along with the stanza saying :—

> "Not marble, nor the gilded monuments
> Of princes, shall outlive this powerful rhyme;
> But you shall shine more bright in these contents
> Than unswept stone, besmear'd with sluttish time,
> When wasteful war shall statues overturn,
> And broils root out the work of masonry;"

for "We see how far the monuments of wit and learning are more durable than the monuments of power or of the hands. For have not the verses of Homer continued twenty-five hundred years or more, without the loss of a syllable or letter; during which time infinite palaces, temples, castles, cities, have been decayed and demolished. The images of men's wits remain in books, exempt from wrong of time, and capable of perpetual renovation."

Such are a few among the round of passages citable to show how, in dealing with one theme, the political poet and "ignorant statesman" by turns employ each other's thoughts and words. The symbolic *Sonnets* are no longer what Ulrici, Dowden, Dyce, and others, despairing of interpretation, declare them to be—"an unsolvable mystery." The innuendo or oblique reading explains Coleridge's difficulty, that "whilst the expression would indicate one sex, the feeling altogether belied it, and secretly wooed and worshipped the other." A mystery will ever remain to direct reading, but not to allegory; the secret yields to parable precisely as the dramas give up their meaning.

This tropical meaning of the *Sonnets*, and their usually erroneous interpretation, is fully manifested by wrong inference often drawn from the two last lines in the 147th verse, running:—

> "For I have sworn thee fair, and thought thee bright,
> Who art as black as hell, as dark as night."

From this picture silly commenters declare the poet's mistress to have been a dark featured woman; when it was her mind and will, not her complexion, that was dark, as plainly appears from the context; and such was Elizabeth's mind and will at the time towards her unhappy favourite for whom Bacon pled in his *Sonnet*, and in so

K

doing placed himself as "a pawn before the Queen;" or, as Kent, to *Lear*, avows :—

> " My life I never held but as a pawn
>   To wage against thine enemies."

The same matter-of-fact literal rendering of the phrases "sweet boy," "lovely boy," applied figuratively to Cupid, as in verse 153, has misled to the greatest blunder in interpreting the *Sonnets*, one that can only bear the saying "Evil to him that evil thinks;" or "To the pure all is pure;" and so is the *Sonnet*.   In the last named verse, 153, the line

> " But at my mistress' eye Love's brand new-fir'd,"

the sentiment agrees with Bacon's allusion to "Her Majesty, whose eyes are the candles of our good days," and so throughout runs the analogy.

The mere idea of staid Francis Bacon inditing a sonnet on any theme is to many minds agreeably ludicrous, and Campbell the cynic, not the poet, thinks the thought only fit for ridicule, and ridicule it he does heartily; and yet the sonnet Bacon says he wrote, and lies like a Cretan on his belly crawling if the sonnet he did not write, could never have been knowingly read by any. But the learned lawyer could not be unaware of Bacon's opinion of the power of poetry to affect the passions; for, in reading for *Lives of the Chancellors*, the biographer undoubtedly read of " some particular writings of an elegant nature touching some of the affections, as anger, comfort under adversity, and other;" and of how "the poets and writers of histories are the best doctors of this knowledge; where we find painted forth with great life, how affections are kindled and incited, and how pacified and restrained; and how again contained from act or further degree; how they disclose themselves, how they work, how they vary, how they gather and fortify, and how they fight one with another, this last being of special use in moral and civil matters, how to set affection against affection, and to master one by another;" or, in other words, to work upon human nature in the very way Bacon aimed to work upon the Queen's better nature to allay her fear of, and assuage her ire against, her erring favourite. Had the critic borne these writings in mind he might have discerned between the face of truth and a false tale, and perceived how Bacon's sonnet gained his end by indirectly working on a strong, though withal womanly, heart; even to perfect success, had the ill-fated friend had wit enough, or been left free enough from evil counsel on the other side, to confess and avoid, as advised, nor vainly justify, resent, or defend, or wilfully hold out to extenuate sedition. There can be no doubt that Bacon did finely hold the magician's bow in the *Sonnet* he wrote to play upon an aching heart, and make the quarrel of lovers the renewal of love, in memory and for rescue, as rescue it would had an errant ring gone right on an errand for mercy. Then would have come pardon, with reintegration; and the still vexed literary world need never wheel and reel in vortices of imagined evil, nor satellites whirl in circlets of borrowed vituperation. What the Queen felt, and meant to condone, is known; yet she, who alone knew all that was said and done, never uttered a reproachful word against the pleading poet, so telling upon her had been his eloquent, though derided, because unread, politico-Platonic *Sonnet.*

Of Bacon's felicity in turning serious prose into playful rhyme, a good example is found in the throwing thoughts on the difference between youth and age into both forms; for, in recounting the varied affections of the mind, the mental moods in youth and age are drawn in contrast alike in treatise and sonnet, in a way one might look for from a poet who sees in a fly entombed in amber "a more than royal tomb;" as any one must see in a moment who reads why

> "Crabbed age and youth
> Cannot live together;"

and compares it with the reasons given for the same antipathies in the history of life and death, a perfect prose sonnet.

Hence the true remark of Macaulay, that "much of Bacon's life was passed in a visionary world, amidst things as strange as any that are described in the Arabian Tales, or in romances," will fitly apply to one who, in a magnificent day-dream, with nothing wild, nothing but what sober reason sanctions, in the regulated effort of a powerful poetic faculty, systematically worked, to save from ruin a falling friend through a love endearing sonnet, conjured by an ever obedient regulated imagination.

VII

THE MANUSCRIPT MYSTERY.

"To publish or suppress what shall be thought fit."

"Yet I was willing they should not be lost."

THE mysterious disappearance of the missing manuscripts from which half the plays in the first *Folio* were printed indicates their authorship. Bacon's *Will* directs certain papers laid away in boxes, cabinets, and presses, to be collected, sealed up, and put away, so as not to have them ready for present publication. Perishing he would prevent, for he knew they could no more be hid than they could be lost. Alluding to the recreations of other studies, he was "not ignorant that those kind of writings would, with less pains and embracement (perhaps), yield more lustre and reputation to my name, than those other which

I have in hand." He therefore sought no untimely anticipation of fame that ordinary men covet. His sudden fatal illness hindered an intended framing of a whole body of philosophy, including Visible History; and the entire neglect by unworthy trustees of a great, varied, and unique estate, because it was heavily encumbered with debt, left many orphan papers uncared-for. Whether any of them were original *MSS.* of plays, or no, it would be idle to inquire, for nobody could tell. That the *MSS.* of the first *Folio*, not entered to other names, may be some day uncupboarded is no unreasonable hope. Other papers thought gone for ever have been recovered, and are now included among his acknowledged ablest works. Many records belonging to noted families, and other papers that were stowed away for safety in cellars of venerable mansions, and even in lofts over old stables, which heirs, enjoying peace after turbulent rebellion, carelessly docketed "worthless papers to be burnt," because as ignorant of their worth as the curate and the barber were of Quixote's library, have been recovered. A similar fate befell the *MSS.* of the first *Folio*, if aught in tradition may be believed. The nominal editors of that volume do not say where they got their manuscript copies; neither do they give the least hint of what they did with them when their loving work was over. What became of the writings is now so fine a mystery as to stimulate the romantic spirit to pleasing invention. In a fiction on the bard's funeral a loving daughter,

"Witty above her sexe,"

is made to show Drayton the coffer where her father kept his writings. But the lamenting poet would not seem to have attached any great value to the writings, for the romancer next alludes to a legend of their being burnt at Warwick, to fulfil Falstaff's saying about "Bakers' wives making bolters of them." But here comes in again the wonted commentary solecism; for Jack talks of beggarly linen shirts—

"Dowlas, filthy Dowlas,"

thin and open in their sieve-like texture; and not of papers, that would not do for flour bolters. The missing manuscripts appear to have been so many times hypothetically burned that it is probable they are still to the fore. They were burnt at Stratford; in the Globe theatre; in London fire; and finally, they were deliberately burnt by their stolid owners by purchase at the playhouse, to hinder rival players from using them! But these silly fables must follow the forgeries that fail to defraud. In spite of imagined facts, invented to get over difficulties better overcome without them, the relics may yet be found hid away in cabinets, presses, hay lofts, or sunk cellars, in some stout old city building that has hitherto withstood the ravages of renovation. In not one of the last *Wills* of the owners of the Globe or other theatre is there a word about manuscript, copyright, book, or literary property of any kind. These endearingly uxorious documents are replete with legal verbiage on pewter plates, brass bowls, beds, warming pans, and trinkets, but never a word on any gift that might betray intellectual leaning in the donor. In this negation all four "fellowes" agree. Money they shared and shared alike; but owned to no manuscript, of which he who sold malt would undoubtedly have made a vendable commodity.

Able judges admit that there are extant compositions with which, though they do not pass under Bacon's name, there is reason to think he had something to do; possibly they are entirely his work. Thirty years after his death a box full of original papers came from the executors of his executor into the hands of one who intended to sort them; but for want of leisure this sorting never took place, and the original papers, whatever they were, "lay undigested in bundles." Evidently writings of Bacon's then existed that cannot now be found.

In his plan of publication, Bacon allots parts of his works to give to the world and circulate from mouth to mouth; the rest he "would pass from hand to hand, with selection and judgment;" for a sober foresight "tells me that the formula of interpretation, and the discoveries made by the same, will thrive better if committed to the charge of some fit and selected minds, and kept private." This plan of the "sugred sonnets among his private friends," he adopts, because he is not hunting for fame, nor looking for gain from his undertaking, meant alone for the good of humanity.

Nothing was heard of the *MSS.* of the first *Folio* until Ben Jonson gathered them together with an urgent appeal to buyers. The reason offered is not enough to account for his being so eager to sell. For seven years Jonson said never a word about the memory of his former friend; and he revived it, without apparent motive, in December, 1623. The widow died four months before, when an ending life interest, if any had been retained for her, would leave the partners free to publish; but they hint no such compact with heirs of any sort. They were as silent in life as they are secret in death. Contrasted with their perfect reticence about copyright, if they had any rights to reserve, Ben Jonson's double editorship of the first *Folio, and* of the minor works of Verulam, all in the same year of 1623, becomes marvellously significant. If Jonson's conduct can be explained in a way neither specious nor merely plausible, but only on fair and reasonable grounds, the plea that he resorted to venial, pardonable artifice to divert attention from the real author becomes conclusive, and the method was as happy as it was at heart honest.

Before sixty years of age, Bacon published little. When the crisis in his fortune came, he had in cabinets and presses many works of careful workmanship ; but, weighty in character as they were, he would not hurriedly publish them, even when they might have got him bread. " My own conjecture is," remarks Mr. Spedding, " that things of more serious import he did not like to publish in an imperfect shape as long as he could hope to perfect them ; but that he owed money to his printer and bookseller, and if such trifles as these would help to pay it, he had no objection to their being used for the purpose." This refers to a few minor works. But when, in 1622, Bacon was driven by biting poverty to this *deliculum surgere*, as he quaintly calls forced publication of *rejicula*—rejected trifles, any *MSS.* of plays would be among what Sir Toby Belch would likewise name *deliculo surgere*, to be sold for what they might fetch, in money, through friendly aid from Jonson, their editor, and dealer with the printer, as general publishing agent for " Egerton's great and unfortunate successor." When Mr. Bosvile got possession of the bundles of manuscripts, hid away in secret corners, and confided by Bacon's will to his care, he carried them with him over to the Hague, whither he went on official duty. From him certain writings relating to morals and politics, and written in English, fell into the hands of Isaac Gruter, who translated some into Latin, while others lay untied as made up by Bacon's own hand. What became of those stray pieces remaining to be accounted for, or what their nature, style, or subject, no biographer ventures to guess. Among the waste rubbish may be the draft of the great organon itself. That it was composed in the tongue the author thought in appears from Rawley's calling it "Instauration," and from Bacon's using the same English term rather than the Latin word *Instauratio*, when telling Mathews how he got along with the work. That whatever Bacon wrote in English was duly turned by helping pens into the general language is well known; and the organon would hardly be wrought upon another rule. The strong good sense is native. One great scholar dressed the thoughts of the *Advancement of Learning* in over-fine Latinity, that Bacon feared the matter might but drown, and therefore he would not have the verbal decoration. What probably was the earliest form of the *Interpretation of Nature* was composed in thorough English, under the cognomen of *Valerius Terminus*, to be annotated by " Hermes Stella," a work eventually turned into Latin like the rest; thus proving that Bacon's early aim was to indite in his native tongue, under fictitious names, keep up anonymity, and eventually transcribe all into Latin, the ever-living tongue.   Hence the twin sets of writings, the logical, ethical, scientific or philosophical, and the dramatic, that have done so much to form English thought, and make England the acme of the world, may now lie hid together in an odd nook of the Teuton land where grew the etymon of her language.

VIII

UNOCCUPIED TIME.

"In what nature of writings to expend my time."

"It may be you shall do posterity good, if out of the carcase of dead and rotten greatness there may be honey gathered for use in future times."

WHAT works occupied Bacon's time between October, 1621, and the winter of 1622, is not fully known. Yet that was the period of his quickest study, celerity in writing, fertility, "conciseness, solidity, and rapidity of style." He was never idle. He had been engaged on a *Life of King Henry VIII.*, but failing health made him "choose some such work as I might compass within days." The projected History following in order after that of *Henry VII.* would have required some months for completion, while the dramatic form would not occupy many days of the most brilliant and fertile period of his career. It also better enabled him to bring in direct allusion to his own adverse fortune.

Of the date of composition of *Henry VIII.*, nothing positive is known. The firing of a gun in acting it is thought to have set fire to the Globe theatre; but this is a hazarded "perhaps," for guns were fired in *Henry V.*, a play that had been often acted. This is all the internal evidence of date; and there is no external proof. On 21st February, 1622, Bacon writes:—"Present my most humble duty to his Highness, who I hope ere long will make me leave *King Henry the Eighth*, and set me on a work in relation of his Highness's heroical adventures." These adventures were met with in the romantic trip of Dog Steenie and Baby Charles to observe *incognito* the Spanish Infanta. About this singular journey Bacon, as one knowing somewhat of the world, was anxious; and, in his almost paternal solicitude for his young friends, he wrote:—" It cannot be but that in my thoughts there should arise many fears or shadows of fears concerning so rare an accident." The noble adventure and the work upon it are related to *The Tempest*, another dateless drama.

During 1621-2 there were intervals of comparative leisure for Bacon sufficiently long to enable *him* to compose dramas that on minute inspection will be found directly bearing on political events involving his own fate. From the close of 1611, when the second edition of the *Essays* was preparing, and after the new version of the Scriptures was ready, with its peculiar *Preface*, ascribed by Scrivener to Miles Smith, but through whose quaint style the mind seems looming that in 1603 began the work, until 1621, official duty filled every minute, save the time spent over the *Instauration*, no drama belonging to any political or social occurrence in the interval being discernible, nor had any one been written for two years before, as already stated; but when again thrown idle from public employment, the ever genial pastime was resumed, as will now be made very plainly to appear, leaving every other explanation by the interpreters

" Clean from the purpose of the things themselves."

IX

JULIUS CÆSAR.

"Let no arbitrary power be introduced."

"It may draw the blow of an assass. against Bu."

THE political allegory of *Julius Cæsar* was written about the same epoch to illustrate the aphorism that absolutism provokes reaction, for "despotism and an abject people are convertible terms;" and "the people of this kingdom love the laws thereof." Bacon would not have the Prince imitate a dictator, but follow the advice of Cicero rather than the example of Cæsar; for Cæsar had sheathed his sword, but never put it off. He would not be a tyrant were not the tag-rag people ready to be slaves: "he would not be a wolf but that he sees the Romans are but sheep: he were no lion, were not Romans "hinds," such as would not be found in England, was the lesson inculcated. Hence the lines—

"With courtesy and with respect enough,
But not with such familiar instances,
Nor with such free and friendly conference
As he had used of old,"

tell the altered tone of the ruling toward the fallen favourite, near enough for autobiography, in one who did only adjure the Prince to

"Stand up against the spirit of Cæsar."

In quite another way Bacon would have his favourite young Prince Charles

"Come by Cæsar's spirit,"

for, with the poet, he held that, " his ambition reserved, Cæsar is the finest spirit of the world." And indeed it is undeniable that Bacon's estimate of Cæsar's character is the same as that given in the drama; in both images the good being picked out from the evil for example. If Cæsar knew how to rule men for their own good and for himself, so was he "given to sports, wildness, and much company," and "in his lust not particular," like the imperious companion of him for whose behoof the image was so presented.

It might now be noted how the word "image" —as in " pulling scarfs off Cæsar's images "— is used in the drama very much as Bacon employs it in his brief account of Cæsar, where he calls that the *Image of Julius Cæsar* that other men would name his character.   At what time Bacon wrote that analysis is quite unknown; though it clearly was meant to read some friend a lesson; and if the favoured one were the · young Prince, then would fitly come to memory the other apt remark about another royal Prince directly alluded to in the *Life of King Henry VII.*, written in 1621, or nearly the date now found to answer the allegory of *Julius Cæsar*.   In *King Richard III.*, the Prince whose fate is chronicled in the *History* for a warning to the living Prince, says :—

> " That Julius Cæsar was a famous man;
> With what his valour did enrich his wit,
> His wit set down to make his valour live:
> Death makes no conquest of this conqueror;
> For now he lives in fame, though not in life,—
> I'll tell you what, my cousin Buckingham,—
> An' if I live until I be a man,
> I'll win our ancient right in France again,
> Or die a soldier, as I liv'd a king."

Here the estimate of the soldier statesman corresponds to that in the paper that was evidently written for an exemplar, to a royal Prince who stood greatly in need of particular guidance, "to allow no arbitrary power to be introduced" into his Government.

The personal bearing of the play is marked enough without heeding the "taking bribes" by one who stood

> "Much condemn'd to have an itching palm ;
> To sell and mart your offices for gold
> To undeservers."

Equally significant are the words :—

> "Shall we now
> Contaminate our fingers with base bribes,
> And sell the mighty space of our large honours
> For so much trash as can be grasped thus ?"

And when Bacon thinks his friend may have heroical spirit to stand out assaults that might have alienated him, and that he is no importuner in asking to be dealt clearly by, his words recall the lines in Cæsar:

> "I do observe you now of late :
> I have not from your eyes that gentleness
> And show of love as I was wont to have :
> You bear too stubborn and too strange a hand
> Over your friend that loves you."

It has been maintained that as Drayton has a line like one in *Julius Cæsar*, his play was the later written, though the reverse may have been the case. Neither is there any evidence that *Julius Cæsar* was known in book or theatre before 1623. And while most of the incidents and many of the words in it are drawn direct from the lives of Cæsar and Brutus, in *Plutarch,* yet this author is very meagre in the account of what occurred after the reading of Cæsar's *Will;* while the play is full of details that could only be obtained from Dio Cassius, whose *History* was never translated into English until long after the date of the drama. Hence the dramatist must have selected materials direct from the only original Greek historian supplying them. There Antony's oration that swayed the mutable people by a breath is given at great length, and in the first person, as paraphrased in the play, while in *Plutarch* that harangue is merely referred to in the third person. In *Dio Cassius* is the phrase " Brouton,—kai su, teknon "— " Brutus, and thou my son ? " forming the famous " Et tu Brute ? " causing so great controversy among commenters. The exclamatory query does not occur in *Plutarch;* but it had already appeared in an earlier play than the extant *Julius*

Cæsar. The ridicule thrown by Ben Jonson on the absurd gait of his theatrical friend mouthing how "Cæsar did never wrong but with just cause," and the solecism of a just cause for doing wrong, shows them intimately acquainted. But in Jonson's words there is an ambiguity that leaves it doubtful whether he were not waiving or evading some matter he did not care to dwell on or disclose. The criticism is wholly unlike his unequivocal praise of Bacon, in whom Jonson saw no literary or intellectual defect, and only moral and intellectual grandeur.

While the English version of *Plutarch* was equally open to Bacon to borrow from as it was free to any one else, so were the *Histories* of Dio Cassius to less well-read writers not open. That Bacon knew these *Histories* in their original form is evident from his freely citing them, as in the dying words of Brutus, in Latin dress truly, and not in Greek; but this he did for uniformity; for in all his works he rarely quotes a Greek author without rendering the passage in Latin; and how readily that could again be turned into heroic metre Bacon's editors show; and what they did with facility could hardly be reckoned beyond the cunning of their master.

And, finally, if Bacon thought Cæsar the finest spirit of the world, so did he likewise hold forth Calphurnia as a pattern not only pure, but even above suspicion. His grand idea of both, as well as his opinion of their betrayal by Decimus Brutus, whom they both cherished, appears in the *Essay* entitled *Of Friendship*, precisely as the poet's opinion appears in the play. For, as the latter says,

> "Break up the Senate till another time,
> When Cæsar's wife shall meet with better dreams,"

the *Essay* repeats it as follows :—" For when Cæsar would have discharged the Senate, in regard of some ill presages, and especially a dream of Calpurnia," (as read by the soothsayer) "this man lifted him gently by the arm out of his chair, telling him he hoped he would not dismiss the Senate till his wife had dreamt a better dream." Now, it will be observed that this allusion to Cæsar in the *Essays* does not occur in the earlier editions, 1597 and 1612, but only in that of 1625; and as it is now affirmed that the extant version of the play was not written before 1621, when men around Bacon "more adored the sun rising than the sun setting," it follows that the passage in the drama and that in the essay were as nearly synchronous in time as they assuredly are identical in sentiment.

There is no name oftener named than Cæsar's in treatise or drama, and in both it is ever coupled to the same heroic ring, always glowing with fervid admiration, barring the inordinate ambition, of the finest embodiment of human greatness and true nobility. But, beside the general plaudit, the native quality and trained art of the man are worked into the drama named after him for a very pointed political allegory applicable to passing momentous events, as can be made appear very plain; for what is the moral taught in the play? Is it not a protest and solemn warning against the growing Cæsarism of the hour, forboding the same final overthrow by the same fatal portents? That the fate of Cæsar was on Bacon's mind almost to an agony in 1621–2–3 is evident from the extract cited from the *Essay* on Friendship; from his brief paper styled the *Image of Cæsar*; and other allusions. He had already warned the

Minister to let no arbitrary power be brought into Government, but to let the Commons be King; he cautioned him against reconciled enemies or discontented friends; and told the ruler, "You must beware of these gen. pardons," made for ostentation or to win popularity, for "it may draw the blow of an assass. against Bu.," as it within five years more verily did. Felton's motive for stabbing Buckingham has never been found; but the assassin was heir of the traitor who posted the papal bull on the London palace, and therefore still one of the traitorous sort towards whom the Minister was displaying what Bacon feared would prove an erring lenity. Hence he wrote in his *Image of Cæsar*:—"Such being the man, the same thing was his destruction at last which in the beginning was his advancement, I mean the desire of popularity. For there is nothing so popular as the forgiveness of enemies: and this it was which, whether it were virtue or art, cost him his life;" and, therefore, the fate that befell Cæsar by "the blow of an assass." was in treatise and drama thus figurately revealed as hanging over his living image.

X

CORIOLANUS.

"There is no hope of mercy in a multitude."

"Our dastard nobles, who
Have all forsook me."

In *Coriolanus* is an example of Bacon's reply to the King, "There is no hope of mercy in a multitude." In conflict with the Commons, a clamour roused by abuse of monopolies rung against the new-made Chancellor, and brought the vindictive enmity of his rivals into under-hand play. To save the King some one had to be sacrificed—"thrown overboard as wares that might be spared." The ægis of the Crown could not shield the menaced Chancellor; but the self-saving law of nature instinctively taught him to save himself. Vowing "innocence as pure as any borne on St. Innocent's day," yet, says he, "if it is absolutely necessary, the King's will shall be obeyed. I am to make an oblation of myself to the King, in whose hands I am as clay, to be made a vessel of honour or dishonour."

The proud Volumnia would have Coriolanus say :

> "I would dissemble with my nature, where
> My fortunes and my friends, at stake, requir'd
> I should do so in honour."

With like loyalty, to save the fortunes of his friends, the King and Minister, the Chancellor made himself an oblation. But, while all applaud the noble sentiment in Volumnia, they revile the vicarious sacrifice in Bacon as abject servility! He had "been no avaricious oppressor of the people." They had been basely trained to accuse him by invention. Yet he would he was still "simply the rarest man i' the world." His "rival's words dis-bench'd him." The enraged Romans were advised to "proceed by process," against Coriolanus, who had to "answer by a lawful form." Bacon would "advise with counsel," and "answer according to the rules of justice." Again, in an impassioned appeal for fair play, the doomed Chancellor says :—"When my enemies are to give fire, am I to make no resistance, and is there to be none to shield me?" In spirit and letter the rebuke is paralleled in—

> " The cruelty and envy of the people
> Permitted by our dastard nobles, who
> Have all forsook me."

And even more emphatic are the warning and prophetic words of Verulam to the King:—" Those who strike at your Chancellor will strike at your Crown. I am the first, I wish I may not be the last sacrifice." That counsel is reiterated by Coriolanus :—

> " Thus we debase
> The nature of our seats, and make the rabble
> Call our cares, fears ; which will in time
> Break ope the locks o' the Senate, and bring in
> The crows to peck the eagles."

The crows did come in to peck the eagles ; and the marvellous prediction at once proves the wisdom and foresight of the true philosophical statesman, and the real authorship of the cognate drama. These obvious analogies are further illustrated by what follows. After he had gone and the nobility were vexed, the masterly Commons among themselves said :—

> " Now we have shown our power,
> Let us seem humbler after it is done,
> Than when it was a-doing."

But the banished leader would not be recalled.
He banished them. He turned his back to find
"a world elsewhere." He had "done with these
vanities." Yet he did assure the King—

> "While I remain above the ground, you shall
> Hear from me still; and never of me aught
> But what is like me formerly."

And so runs on the remarkable resemblance.
When Bacon's study became his exchange, and
his pen his factor for the use of his talent, he
had no desire to stage himself, nor pretension
but for the comfort of a private life. He had
found pleasure in comfort, but no comfort in
pleasure. "Yet," in sorrow he says, " I will ever
be at God's and the King's call: malcontent
or busybody I scorn to be." And he adds, in
an offering to the King: " My desire to serve
your Majesty is of the nature of the heart, that
will be *ultimum moriens* with me."

> " The King hath killed his heart."

Like Coriolanus, the outcast in banishment would
continue to be his country's benefactor. Although
Bacon " did not like the word people " yet he
" would have kings give their subjects good

laws;" while he as vigorously hated "the meaner sort of politiques, that are sighted only to see the worst of things, and think that laws are but cobwebs," as ever Lear hated the courtier to whom he said :—

> " Get thee glass eyes;
> And, like a scurvy politician, seem
> To see the things thou dost not."

To mirror his fidelity in dramatic allegory is the political motive of that reflective drama. This conclusion cannot be affected by any fanciful chronology of a play unheard of before 1623. An assumed allusion to a dearth in England in 1610 made that event be fixed upon for the date of the play. But the reference to a famine in the land, and at the time of the hero of the story, is more accurate and appropriate, requiring no absurd assumption.

XI

KING HENRY VIII.

If contemplative, 1. Going on with the story of H. the 8th.

"I am the shadow of poor Buckingham."

THAT *King Henry VIII.* was written after Bacon's fall is evident from the language and allusions of Buckingham and Wolsey, and the grieved Commons, making biographies of the bygone visible allegories of current history, wherein all saw themselves reflected, in mightiness meeting misery, for "crimes of insolency and ingratitude seldom have their doom adjourned to the world to come."

The fate of Verulam is plainly read in Buckingham's words—

"I had my trial,
And must needs say, a noble one."

"Both
Fell by our servants, by those men we lov'd most,"

Bacon fell by his servants. Spies they were in his own house, fed to ferret out constructive cases to betray their master. Rising to salute him, he bowed and said, "Sit down, my masters; your rise has been my fall."

> "O, good! convey?—conveyors are you all,
> That rise thus nimbly by a true king's fall."

In astute, dissembling Williams, the profligate ecclesiarch who procured the vacant seal, is a man "not propp'd by ancestry," "nor call'd for high feats done to the Crown." He "spider-like, out of 's own web," "buys for him a place next to the King," exactly as bought the cunning hierocrat. Indeed, "this holy fox, or wolf, or both," ravening and subtle, who had many a "brown wench lie kissing in his arms," "paid ere he promised: whereby his seat was granted ere it was ask'd;" for in this very manner was the evicted Chancellor's office given over Bacon's head as the price of infamy to the new lord keeper. Verulam, as "the King's attorney, urg'd on the examinations, proofs, confessions of divers witnesses," to bring them forward to confute this "devil-monk that made the mischief."

In the same manner Bacon pled hard to have his case thoroughly investigated. He too wished to be allowed to except to the witnesses brought against him, to move questions for their cross-examination, and likewise to produce his own witnesses for discovery of the truth, and was denied!

When the Lord Cardinal is informed that all he had done of late "by your power legatine, within this kingdom, fall within the compass of a *præmunire*," the legal term employed is that defined by Bacon to vindicate the royal prerogative against an attempt to appoint to a benefice by *commendam*, setting up a court legatine over the Court of King's Bench, to entrench on regal right. Bacon thus in the play reminded the King of the important service he had rendered to England in confirming her right and title to independent monarchy. Doubtless he also hinted at the

> " Stubborn answer
> About the giving back the great seal to us."

In thus alluding to his fealty there are the ever recurring words,

> " Commend me to his Grace.
> . . . My vows and prayers
> Yet are the King's."

And if any doubt remain in the mind of the reader of the real motive and author of the play, let the doubter read and compare the *Fortunate Memory of Elizabeth* with the final oration of Cranmer on the same theme. That speech is quite evidently a vaticination after the fact, for how could Cranmer know the infant would live, and die an unspotted lily, a virgin Queen? The lines beginning with,

> " Nor shall this peace sleep with her : but as when
> The bird of wonder dies, the maiden phœnix
> Her ashes new create another heir
> As great in admiration as herself,"

are but the counterpart or complement of that passage in the *Memory* saying, " Her death was followed by two posthumous felicities, more lofty and august perhaps than those which attended her in life—her successor and her memory."

In 1621-2 Bacon often writes how the sparks of his affection are quick, under the ashes of his fortune, to revive again. And so all throughout, in feeling and expression, the prose oration and the dramatic dialogue, even to naming Anne Bullen, not Boleyn, are the same. No allusion is made in the play to Anne Bullen's fate, but Bacon refers to it in an *Apophthegm* written at

M 2

the time; in the play any notice of it would have been away from the purpose of the allegory.

Lastly, and to make an end where no end is, in this remarkable parallel, when reading the resigned words of the Lord Cardinal's wailing valedictory to King Henry VIII., it is impossible to refrain from comparing them with the fallen Lord Chancellor's final appeal to King James. They also were words of "the prime man of the state," left, weary and old with service, "to the mercy of a rude stream." And as he exclaims, "Why should I speak of these things, which are now vanished, but only the better to express the downfall?" adding, "I hope God above, of whose mercies towards me, both in my prosperity and my adversity," so does the other say,

> " Had I but serv'd my God with half the zeal
> I serv'd my King, he would not in mine age
> Have left me naked to mine enemies."

But even still more explicitly Bacon writes in September, 1621, evidently with Henry VIII. in his mind :—"Cardinal Wolsey said that if he had pleased God as he pleased the King, he had not been ruined. My conscience saith no such thing; for I know not but in serving you I have served God in one. But it may be, if I had pleased men as I have pleased you, it would have been better with me."

In sad soliloquy and bitter retrospect, each fallen Chancellor could and did say of an ungrateful King, that he "left me in the mire of an abject and sordid condition in my last days."

Again, the prologue to *King Henry VIII.* recites the trivial notions of the plays as merry shows for idlers to "see away their shilling richly;" and adds that they are not meant to make frivolity laugh at sheer buffoonery, as do dull stage capers of the time; but are rather intended for

"The first and happiest hearers of the town,"

who are to think they see

"The very persons of our noble story
As they were living,"

and from their fate learn

"How soon this mightiness meets misery."

This prologue may have been endited by Ben Jonson while editing the first *Folio.* It agrees with the spirit of the then recently completed *History of Henry VII.* This too shows "The proper object of *History* is to reproduce such an image of the past that the actors shall seem to live and the events to pass before our eyes." In this respect the *History* is matchless. It warned the young Prince of a growing Cæsarism. His forefather governed by personal rule. The author "took him to the life," for it was "not amiss" that the youth "should also see one of these ancient pieces." That *History* drew a forecast of what befell a monarch who would not contentedly go with the times and wisely let the Commons be King. Like his forefathers, he too would be his own Prime Minister. Firm adherence to the *thorough* tradition of his house showed him how soon this mightiness meets misery; that even in an absolute monarch offences of presumption are the greatest.

The *History of the Reign of King Henry VII.* is dramatic. Flat as are the incidents narrated in "The Story of England," the tale could readily have been thrown into dramatic form, like the historic play with which it is so intimately and immediately connected. But then, that alteration of form would have divulged the secret of their common authorship; this was not wished, and the change in form was not adopted.

The *King Henry VIII.*, therefore, is evidently another ancient piece revived in verse rather than in prose as at first designed, and made visible in dramatic allegory, to illustrate the passing phase of then current history. All arguments on the date of the play are mutually contradictory, not one being apodictic, but leaving it to be deduced from internal evidence, as is now attempted. Next follows the retrospect in the grand climacteric, when the life review forewarns a loved protegé, the favourite young prince, whom England vainly slaughtered for a righteous principle, and then restored in his son, just to show the world how soon fanatic as well as regal

"Mightiness meets misery."

XII

THE TEMPEST.

"The King was wont to say : if good for anything, for great volumes."

"Knowing I lov'd my books, he furnish'd me,
From mine own library, with volumes that
I prize above my dukedom."

ALTHOUGH *The Tempest* is an elaborately finished play, for which no origin has ever been fairly assigned, its aim as a political allegory is very manifest. The poem is admittedly composed in the poet's latest style. The tale on which the main plot is founded, "for, on some tale it was undoubtedly founded," has hitherto "eluded the grasp of commentators." This dubiety leaves inquiry free. With leave to roam over the field of romance for a prototype, fancy need draw no ideal inference, nor let ingenuity force analogy beyond reason in finding out the real in imagery, and give to airy nothing a local habitation and a name.

Briefly defined, *The Tempest* may be called a dirge on a life-wreck, in a mournful calm after a storm. In the wail of the dying wind a moan is heard, warning a youth gaily embarking on the voyage of life, and at flood-tide, to steer clear of the shallows that bound every life venture, and, if unheeded, leave it stranded in miseries.

In February, 1623, the young Prince Charles, with his gay comrade, sailed from London, for Madrid, on their romantic wooing cruise. Their Æolus, "left desolate till their return, set him on a work in relation to his Highness's heroical adventure." Loving the gallant pair, and knowing somewhat of the world, it could not be but that in Bacon's thoughts "there should arise many fears or shadows of fears concerning so rare an accident" as that which befell them on crossing the river at Gravesend, disguised, near midnight, when, on offering the waterman gold for his ferry across the stream, the rough tar, little knowing whom he had aboard, took them for runaways, and tried to detain them as man-o'-war prisoners.

When they returned in October, or eight months after sailing, Bacon wrote to the Prince that he had finished *Henry VIII.*, not as a History at length, but in a form he had compassed within days, and adds :—"I would I could do your Highness's journey any honour with my pen. It began like a fable of the poets : but it deserveth all in a piece a worthy narration." The worthy narrative took the form of *The Tempest.* Relieved from the main labour of translating his great works into Latin, Bacon had during the autumn of 1623 leisure to spare for an occasional piece like a drama, that he "might compass within days." The mental agony he had lately gone through, without brightening hope, brought the end of his days a good deal nearer, in health if not in years ; and the genius, more brilliant than ever, fell into the valedictory mood, ready to lay down his pen and his art.

Seeing the drift of "reconciled enemies and discontented friends" on whom he relied—"dissimulation, falsehood, baseness, and envy in the world, and so many idle clocks going in men's heads"—he despaired of any waif of fortune being borne towards him on a turning tide. During the absence of the voyagers he had ridden at anchor; but his cables were now quite worn. All his tackling had been in their means. In these he thought he had an anchor well out; for though "fortunes be above the thunder and storms of inferior regions, yet nevertheless to hear the wind and not to feel it will make one sleep the better." At this period of his wrecked fortunes all his similes were nautical. He wrote: "When I enter into myself I find not the materials of such a tempest as is come upon me." He was "compared to a mariner, who, being wrecked on an island with a rocky and savage shore, on going into the interior, finds it covered with beautiful verdure, watered with clear streams, and abounding with all sorts of delicious fruits," much like Prospero's fabled island. This singularly apt similitude was drawn after Bacon had been cut adrift by crafty Williams, who in the mutiny wanted him pitched overboard as "ware that might be spared" to ease the lurching ship of state in the rising storm. The victim was jettisoned, but the ship was not saved. Like Prospero, he was not dismayed, but could well "be cheerful, sir," in all his sorrows. "Pardon me to be merrie, however the world goeth with me." He was "as a man overthrown by a tempest."

This idea of shipwreck has ever floated in the thoughts of biographers, as in his own. After he had gone from the Tower, "when in the middle of his fullest sea and fairest weather, he found himself suddenly among the breakers." The catastrophe left him in "an infirm health and the settling the poor planks of my wracks;" yet, he adds, "in the beginning of my trouble, when in the midst of the tempest, I had a kenning of the harbour which I hope now I am entering into."

Thus markedly were all his metaphors water-borne about harbours, wracks, planks, cables, anchors, tackling, and *Tempests.* Yet he would be no "abbey-lubber." He too was a man of books, and only wanted a cell to retire into for study. That liberty he was denied. It was "feared that literature itself would be disgraced if a convict were permitted to become author." Only in one who was "for liberal arts without a parallel" can Prospero be identified. He too had a brother Antonio, who was "perfected how to grant suits," and held "both the key of office and of officer," and took "upon him the manage of my state," while he, "rapt in secret studies," and "neglecting worldly ends, dedicated all to closeness, and the bettering" of his mind. They were all his study. For him, poor man, his library was dukedom large enough. When "i' the dead of darkness" hurried to the Tower, a noble one,

> "Of his gentleness,
> Knowing I lov'd my books, he furnish'd me,
> From mine own library, with volumes that
> I prize above my dukedom."

The banished book-worm did actually get books in that way. He too "studied books rather than men." He had read his leaf, and so with him Prospero might say, "Something I have been, and somewhat I have read." At court each had

> "An enemy
> To me inveterate."

Besides, each had a staunch friend in "an honest old counsellor." One had Gonzalo; the other Tobie Mathews, who each could be merry, and weigh sorrow with comfort; and, along with Bacon, say, and indeed many a time, as is already cited, repeat,—

<blockquote>
" I' the commonwealth I would by contraries
Execute all things."
</blockquote>

To Bacon, who would fain have gone with the voyagers to give them careful advice, Mathews, then living in Spain, was " to me another myself," in whom they "find a wise and able gentleman, and one that will bend his knowledge of the world, which is great, to serve the young men," precisely as Gonzalo tends on Ferdinand.

At the time of *The Tempest* the main aim of great men was to knock each other out of power into the Tower, and secure their heads as hostages. The allusions in the drama certainly apply with force and precision to the victim then pinched in the devil dungeon. The Swan of Avon never was so caged; but at the time Bacon's daily call was *Pro Spero* for freedom. Applicable allusions to persons are held valid proofs of authorship. At that date Bacon, "infirm and old," looked around and above him, and "pardon'd the deceiver" when by a parable he revealed the secret of his life work. Then the spirit creative that did " resemble the angels " promised his spirit Ariel early liberty. Retiring to his cell, "where every third thought shall be my grave," he was in the right frame of mind to bequeath :—"My name and memory I leave to foreign nations, and to my own countrymen after some time be passed over." He was in no hurry to give them "a thread of his own life ;" but they begin to think and say :—

"Please you, further."

In 1620 the "everliving benefit to nature" was conferred, and in a year the grateful children of nature put their benefactor in the Tower, through

"That foul conspiracy
Of the beast Caliban,"

who, with pains had been made to speak, taught each hour one thing or other, when the savage knew not his own meaning, but would gabble like a thing most brutish, and had his purposes endowed with words that made them known, exactly as Bacon had trained his rival and inveterate enemy Coke, in whom, therefore, is found the prototype of the treacherous servant monster. He, like a "firebrand in the dark," had told confederates how to "brain him," having first seized his books and "brave utensils;" and, by way of retribution, himself got "pinch'd" in the cupboard where England kept her political skeleton.   Here indeed is a poetical picture of the lifelong vindictive acts of Coke, and the bitter invective of Bacon, true to the life.

In the setting of the portrait is a recollection of the toil of the slave spirit Ariel for the "blue-ey'd hag" Sycorax, the heartbreaker, to whom Bacon

> .   .   .   " wast a spirit too delicate
> To act her earthy and abhorred commands.
> Refusing her grand hests, she did confine thee,
> By help of her more potent Ministers,
> And in her most unmitigable rage,
> Into a cloven pine; within which rift
> Imprison'd, thou didst painfully remain
> A dozen years; within which space she died."

For thus railed he at her memory who preferred Caliban, and made the brute his tormentor.

These relations of feigned names in fable to real names in fact lead to a true interpretation of an ambiguous phrase in *The Tempest* that has hitherto baffled the skill of all interpreters to guess at or explain—a phrase, moreover, which has misled everyone to assume an erroneous date and origin for the play.   In the "still vex'd Bermoothes" is a needless yet perpetual puzzle.

The phrase is usually taken to be an allusion to the islands of the Bermudas, where ships belonging to Somer's fleet were wrecked in 1610; and to that catastrophe and date *The Tempest* is assigned. But neither Bermuda nor Lampedusa is meant. Name and phrase are borrowed and modified from the like sounding " still disturbed Bermeja," the enchanted island in *Amadis of Gaul*, the same probably that Bacon alludes to in his *Fortunate Memory of Queen Elizabeth*, where, of her wooing and courting even beyond the natural age for such vanities, he says they are much like the accounts we find in romances of the Queen in the blessed islands, and her court and institutions, who allow of amorous admiration, but forbid desire. Though Mr. Spedding is not able to learn what romance is here alluded to, it doubtless is that named. This romance was a great favourite of Bacon's, and he often alludes to it, as when he declares the laws of England are not taken from *Amadis of Gaul.* The island was England, to which the old Portuguese romance refers. There abode the enchanting daughter of the Necromancer whose miracles favour the lives of Amadis and Oriana much as Prospero's miracles aid Ferdinand and Miranda. Both tales set forth the character of a perfect knight in the virtues of courage and chastity. In each tale a Magician, an Enchantress, a Hermit, and a Dwarf appear; and after a tempest and shipwreck on an unknown rock, appalling mariners, with lights on the yards and masts, work miracles during the adventures of two knights, ending in the overthrow of the enchantments, and marriage of Amadis and Oriana, Ferdinand and Miranda. The old tale was written for a Ferdinand of Spain, as was the new. At the date of the later written *Tempest* tale Bacon's mind ran on a miracle that could be performed for him. Writing to Count Gondomar, then in Spain, about what he had done for a King and a Prince, he says :—" Since your Lordship hath had power to work these miracles in a public fortune, it is a much less matter for you to work a miracle in the fortune of a private friend; and since your Lordship hath power and I have faith, a miracle is soon wrought, if your Lordship think it worth the stretching forth your noble hand," as would be done for an unfortunate by chivalric Amadis or generous Prospero.

Combined with the tale of the noble adventure, like a fable of the poets, about a shipwreck in England, and the rest of the fleet dispersed to the " Mediterranean flote," is a significant interlude on the worship of Paphos.

After Prospero adjures Ferdinand to be " more abstemious," and hears his vow made on the " white cold virgin snow upon his heart," the spirit Ariel is called upon to " bring in a corollary," when Iris, Ceres, and Juno enter and recite the Paphian mysteries. Here the poet adorned no mere lifeless abstraction. His art had a direct object and literal meaning. In living character the scene revealed the sacred and the beautiful. A favourite youth had erewhile given " dalliance too much the rein " with the fair daughter of Rutland, though it did not melt his " honour into lust." But he being about to look upon another Miranda, in the Infanta, " Dog Steenie " needed admonition in,—

<blockquote>
" Look thou be true ;
The strongest oaths are straw
To the fire i' the blood."
</blockquote>

The warning in the poem is an idealized reiteration of advice offered to Villiers by Bacon, "as an hermit rather than a courtier," not long before the storm that broke over the voyagers when crossing the Thames struck the poet, "sad and discreet," with the thought uttered in the first breaking of *The Tempest*.

At what date *The Tempest* was written there is not a jot or tittle of external evidence to show; nor any proof that the play was known to exist prior to 1623. All attempts to prove it to have been known in 1611 have failed. Entries in the Record of Court Revels, said to refer to it, "have lately been found gross forgeries." Similar entries of the alleged acting of the play in 1613 are in "an imperfect record" apparently no better. A play of the same title may possibly have been acted, but nothing exists to indicate identity with the play now extant. Many plays with similar titles existed before the true one. Supposed allusions to it in the "tales, tempests, servant-monsters, and drolleries," in Ben Jonson's Induction to *Bartholomew Fair*, are now found quite irrelevant, they being evidently mere sarcasms at "admirable fooling" amongst monsters exhibited for vulgar wonderment at the great popular carnival. Testimony now offered leaves not a tittle of remaining doubt about the conclusion that *The Tempest*, when it was printed for the first time in 1623, as the first of the series in the first *Folio*, was then the final touch fresh from the wand of the Magician, who then laid down his àrt and buried his book. The play is a pure trilogy made up of autobiography, of a Paphian warning to two young friends, and of an example of chivalry in the Child of the Sea, to be emulated by the living and then true Prince of Wales, who was likewise the veritable Child of The Lady of the Sea.

XIII

TIMON OF ATHENS.

"Last scene of all
That ends this strange, eventful history."

"A young man reverences his superiors;
An old man finds out their faults."

THAT *Timon of Athens* came immediately after *The Tempest* is critically allowed, from the ring of the old storm still resounding. It too is a trilogy; but the three separate parts or plots and groups of characters in it are imperfectly blended, leaving a crude, ill-unified combination that makes critics fancy the play no work of one author, but a patchwork by many writers. Differing from the plaintive life review that had just gone before it, Timon is only ironical when not intensely sarcastic, mating two plays by antithesis. Indeed, Timon is told by the real cynic Apemantus that his sour, cold habit is put on to feign *Misanthropos*, and treat a fawning crowd derisively. If this were the intent, Timon imitates or repeats the affected severity that makes the *Temporis Partus Maximus* unpopular. The play is replete with thoughts and feelings expressed akin to plaints abounding in Bacon's letters and papers written between 1621 and 1623, when all hope of regaining lost honour, dignity, or office finally fled. Then he in despair sought a cell or a cave to retire to as did Timon, and, like him, to be attended only by a devoted steward, whose faith and worth are true to the character of Flavius, even to idiomatic wording. Just like Flavius was faithful Thomas Meautys. That such another pair of stewards never did meet would be a rather wide belief; but that they did appear together in 1623 is certain. Each belonged to the " noblest of the noble order of loyal servants, loyal to the full extent of his means and abilities, in adversity as in prosperity, in disgrace as in honour, loyal through life and beyond it, the creditor who never ceased to be friend." Such was Steward Meautys, and even so is Flavius to the

> " Poor honest lord, brought low by his own heart,
> Undone by goodness."

Both "bleed inwardly" for his unhappy lord and master, as he vows,

> " I'll ever serve his mind with my best will ;
> Whilst I have gold, I'll be his steward still."

As Flavius behaves in the play, so did, in 1621-2, Thomas Meautys, in all things true. The scene and the colloquy of the servants in the play repeat the scene and colloquy among the servants in the lobby—the "lobbies once fill'd with tendance"—of the whilom munificent Chancellor, now alternately visited and forsook "by all the noblemen about the town ;" but who would yet in solitude and ruin give advice as when he held the seal, and be as ever "the old man still." For did not Bacon say, what Timon does repeat :

> " But yet I love my country ; and am not
> One that rejoices in the common wreck,
> As common bruit doth put it."

Like almost all the other plays that were printed for the first time in the 1623 *Folio*, and of which no reference records the acting at any theatre, public or private, great uncertainty exists as to the date when this play was written. Hence one passage in the servant's speech is called corrupt from the original text, an interpolation to hit off some lord who fairly "strives to appear foul! takes virtuous copies to be wicked," in the wicked reign of Charles. But if the play were really not written until 1623, no such gratuitous assumption is needed, for the alleged spurious passage would then be *e re nata*, an actual direct application to a living personage, and the passage perfectly genuine, as Coleridge could not have failed to perceive had he dreamt of the true authorship.

The same premises would enable all who, with Malone, think the author could have had no help from Lucian, "there being then no translation of the dialogue that relates to this subject," for the real writer would need no such aid. Of the *MS.* comedy on the subject of *Timon*, printed by Mr. Dyce, that able editor writes :—" That our poet had any acquaintance with it I much doubt ; for it certainly was never performed in London, being a drama intended solely for the amusement of an academic audience." That comedy was most probably written by him who in 1623 remodelled his own earlier work for later political purposes. Hence an ample explanation of many otherwise irreconcilable difficulties in the text of both productions. Hence also a reason for the passage so perfectly descriptive of the careless good lord and his careful steward :—

> " O, my good lord,
> At many times I brought in my accounts,
> Laid them before you ; you would throw them off,
> And say you found them in mine honesty."

> " My dear-lov'd lord,
> Though you hear now—too late—yet now 's a time,
> The greatest of your having lacks a half
> To pay your present debts."

This is merely repetition of many conversations between Meautys and Bacon, on the *res augusti domi*. That the words would equally well apply to any spendthrift who

> " Takes no account
> How things go from him,"

and who feared not false times when he did feast, is undeniable in general ; but it is equally undoubted that, taken along with all other circumstances, they serve to identify the particular steward who showed to his most worthy master, merely in love,

> " Duty and zeal to your unmatchèd mind,
>   Care of your food and living,"

at a time when his most honoured lord wanted food and a cave to live in, in pure affection and not

> " For any benefit that points to me,
>   Either in hope or present."

In brief, it is impossible not to recognize the picture, for nothing in art was ever so graphic. The background can be freely filled in with an infinite variety of parallel passages, to repeat which would only be weary iteration to readers of the compared originals, while full detail, however convincing, might fail to edify the indifferent, enough being done to prove something far beyond mere general likeness arising from casual coincidence.

In " The Differences between Youth and Old Age" is enumerated every distinguishing detail in the seven ages of man, till in old age the humours are phlegmatic and melancholy, and the blood is cold, crude, and watery, with a tendency to decrepitude and a three-legged animal, death ; just as in

> " These old fellows,
> Their blood is cak'd, 'tis cold, it seldom flows ;
> And nature, as it grows again toward earth,
> Is fashion'd for the journey, dull and heavy."

If the reader fail to find wherefrom the passage comes, then the *History of Life and Death* cannot have been made a study.

In the scene in the Senate House with Alcibiades pleading, there is a commentary on Buckingham's futile efforts to intercede for Bacon with the Lords, and secure a mitigation of the severe sentence, the sorest point in the great grief that provoked the invective on men obdurate and vindictive. With wonted prescience Bacon foresaw the time not distant when the Senate would gladly again hail him as leader, because he well knew they could not get on without his aid in that capacity. And just as he warned the vacillating King how they who strike at his Chancellor will strike at his Crown, and the daws come in to peck the eagles, and foresaw the blow of the assassin that stabbed the reckless Buckingham, so did Bacon foresee

> " The senators with one consent of love
> Entreat thee back to Athens."

The public body seldom does play the recanter, but well the injured leader knew how the Senate would one day yield to retribution. In that he was prophetic. When the deputation waited on him to enter the new Parliament as captain, they found him in his cell writing his epitaph, preparing for the inevitable change from his long sickness; when to their request he replied, " Come not to me again, for I have done with these vanities," for such were in sentiment and feeling the latest words of each misanthrope to the unfeeling yet relenting politicians.

XIV

SUMMARY OF PROOFS.

" Be govern'd by your knowledge."

" The sovereignty of man lieth hid in knowledge."

HAVING given ample proof of the Baconian authorship of the Renascence Drama, it will now be in order to consider Ben Jonson's relation to the work.

That he, the ripe scholar, rare genius, and outspoken, blunt, good friend, with a warm heart grieved for an honoured man, could keep a secret sorrowfully, says more for native goodness than maumish rant about deceit can touch or qualify. To be made in terrible hours of stricken sorrow the trusted confidant of the renowned one, whom the Fates had spun out of their softest and their finest wool, would hold him bound in honour to succour the broken bankrupt on the verge of actual starvation. To that sore flight was the fallen Verulam in 1622 abruptly brought. The sources of his income were suddenly dried up. The spent hour-glass was in great extremity. He was no longer "master of pens" as he had been. "The poor remnants which I had of my former fortunes in plate or jewels I have spread upon poor men unto whom I owed, scarce leaving myself bread." His highest ambition now was for a cell to retire to, and "bare means to live out of want and die out of ignominy." He that had borne a bag feared lest he might have to wear a wallet. He who would live to study had to study to live. Yet he had no desire to stage himself. "Malcontent or busybody I scorn to be." Such were the words of the "bank rowt" who had no other means of living, or of getting a bit of bread for himself and his family, than the casual sale of bygone literary work. To gather together saleable scraps, "*quelques opuscules*," as Bouillet names them, was in 1622–3 Ben Jonson's special work, while Hobbes and Herbert were translating and preparing more elaborate scientific and philosophical writings for publication. From those particulars, and also from a remark of Mr. Spedding's, that about this time "Ben Jonson, who had seen something of Bacon off the stage, though we do not know how much," it is tolerably evident that, during the year before the publication of the first *Folio*, Ben Jonson was assisting in the twofold capacity of editor of Bacon's minor works and the grand dramatic volume !   In noticing that the definition of dramatic poetry, already referred to, first appeared in the Latin form or translation of the *Advancement of Learning*, in 1623, Mr. Spedding observes :—" It is a curious fact that these remarks on the character of the modern drama were probably written and were certainly first published in the same year which saw the first collection."   But the added " doubt whether Bacon had ever heard" of that drama, which so perfectly fulfils his own definition, hardly seems quite tenable.   Nor does John Chamberlain's silence about the plays, in his letters to Dudley Carleton, fairly imply, as is affirmed, Bacon's equal ignorance of their existence.   Indeed, the contrary is the more valid argument ; for if Bacon had to maintain the character of the ignorant author, as he long maintained that of " ignorant statesman," it would be his continual study to preserve anonymity. To make the plea good, it is assumed that many plays, including *Coriolanus*, *Othello*, *The Tempest*, and others printed for the first time in 1623, had long before appeared as novelties. But this involves the disputed point, and implies an affirmative of the assertions questioned. That Bacon could have been ignorant of the Renascence Drama, even allowing him not its author, is incredible. He who was so active in preparing masques, devices, and revels for court entertainment would hardly be indifferent to *The Merry Wives* or *Midsummer Night's Dream*, and could not but hear Lord Cobham's complaint against the playwriter who lampooned his forefather. But there is positive evidence of Bacon's cognizance of the plays in their political relation. The acting of *Richard II.* by the partisans of Essex is referred to by him; and the play was written several years before. That the famous deposition scene was meant to warn Elizabeth of the fate impending over her is made plain by the reference, in Bacon's account of the arraignment, to the way in which King Richard II. was betrayed by one who presented himself with three humble reverences, and in the end was deposed and put to death. Nor is there any reason to suppose it was some obsolete play that had been furbished up for the seditious pastime.   The objection of the player that the performance would involve loss, and the guarantee of Sir Gilly Merrick against that contingency, because, as Camden remarks, the cautelous player spoke of an obsolete play, is no proof that it was not the genuine one with the doubtful part left out to humour the Queen, who got naturally alarmed with rumours of sedition.

While occupied in the double work of editing the first *Folio* and Bacon's minor works, Ben Jonson wrote of his friend that he "could never condole in a word or syllable to him, as knowing that no accident could do harm to virtue, but rather serve to make it manifest."   Both were heart-wrung, and in the mood to declare that "The King has killed his heart."   This apt phrase is interpolated in *Henry V.*, in the *Folio;* for it is in no earlier quarto.   It appeared in 1623, when Jonson was editing the *Folio*, and condoling with Bacon on the King's cruelty.

With these feelings of kind sympathy, true friendship, and fealty for a wronged unfortunate, to say nothing of admiration for genius, where lay the harm of using a name to make a book sell, and yet conceal the anonymous author? Jonson knew that popularity always goes by the first claim, and felt it did no hurt to the memory of the owner of this loaned name, often aforetime so lent. The long-forgotten writings lying perdue in cabinets and presses were brought forth and printed. To make the book sell, an urgent, almost abject appeal is made. " Whatever you do, buy," implores Jonson, who well might have added, " for I would get my friend bread." The same appeal was made by Rawley to King James, to hurry back the proofs of *Henry VII.*, for " the stationer's fingers itch to be selling." Money had been advanced on both works, and the trader wanted quick return. So great was the hurry that Bacon read no proofs. Hence the errors left for mending critics. The blurs of haste are due to no illiterate labour. There was no blot on the copy, yet the book is full of blunder. The work was rushed through the press in a way that made mistakes unavoidable. Of the printer's dealings with the owner of the MSS., nothing is known, beyond anxiety to bring

the commodity quickly to market.   Hence could
Jonson tell of Bacon,

" And in the midst
Thou stand'st as if some mystery thou didst."

The very dedication of the *Folio* to Lord
Montgomery is a link in the chain of proof.
He was the mutual friend then acting for Lady
Bacon and Meautys with Buckingham, through
the trials of 1622. " There is no honester man
in court than Montgomery." " Montgomery is
an honest man and good observer."   These are
entries at the time in Bacon's private diary.
They reveal friendly esteem and confidence. Ere
Essex fell, to Southampton went the honour of
a dedication of the *Venus and Adonis,* and
Lucrece, the *Sonnets* being dedicated to " W. H.,"
and the early quartos having no patron.   But
although in 1623, when the first *Folio* appeared
with sixteen plays either quite new or at all
events never before heard of, Southampton had
long been restored to royal favour, the old intimacy
between him and Bacon was not renewed, and
the new volume found a truer and more genial
friend.   Indeed, an old foe was revived to new
enmity.   He who led Essex away from Bacon's

advice reminded the Lords of the "convict" Bacon's failure to comply with their order. Had he kept quiet, they would have been silent; the "felon" Bacon might have peaceably printed his book; but the unbeheaded traitor was not to be baulked of the victim caught in the toil. In ignorance and stolidity cemented with malice, Southampton stands prototype for Trinculo. Nursing an old grievance, he waited for revenge. Feeling another storm brewing, he heard it sing in the wind. If it thundered as before, he knew not where to hide his head. When the storm again came, the craven crept for shelter under the gabardine of Coke, "the Huddler." As of old, he felt as Trinculo did, when creeping under Caliban's skirt, how "misery acquaints a man with strange bed-fellows." The pair made the typified four-legged monster conspiring in the Lords' against Bacon, as Trinculo and Caliban aim at Prospero in the allegory.

Therefore to Southampton the *Folio* is not dedicated, the honour being reserved for the former confidant, "W. H." William Herbert, Earl Pembroke, and Philip Herbert, Earl Montgomery, at the time when their relative, Sir

Henry Herbert, was Master of the Revels, and another relative, George Herbert, was a co-editor of Bacon's works. The two Earls were of the royal household, one being Lord Chamberlain, and are called in the *Folio* as in Bacon's *Diary*, " our singular good lords," and all would help Jonson to go through formality and enable him to conceal the author.

If Bacon were the author of these dramas, why, it is asked, should he conceal the fact ? To answer this natural query requires a short study of his idiosyncrasy. An amiable and ingenuous mind gladly gives counsel without parade or ostentation. Knowing that to be his peculiar trait, his wish for privacy becomes at once credible and laudable. He says :—" I must confess my desire to be, that my writings should not court the present time, or some few places, in such sort as might make them either less general to persons, or less permanent in future ages."   " He was not for an age, but for all time."   Besides, it must be remembered that, much as Bacon prized the theatre, he more highly admired the palace of the mind. There he reverently approached, and enters in his own name. Works of nature set forth the Workman's skill, but do not portray the image of their Maker. In "beholding it in the soul of man as in a mirror," the worshipper reflected that knowledge which alone is not deficient. The Scriptures directly term man "the image of God." Polity required a parable; the spiritual part of man needed no device. Writing to his intimate friend, Toby Mathews, he refers to a "little work of my recreation." That was in 1609, and no new play appeared between then and the printing of *Othello* in 1621. About 1609, Mathews bantered his friend on writing many things "under another name." The practice was familiar, and fair, honourable, self-denying magnanimity.

It is often painfully argued that the alleged poet had enjoyed ample opportunity to learn enough of Greek, Latin, French, and Italian to fit him for the work, eking out shortcomings by help of translations—that is, had to acquire knowledge by ordinary modes of vulgar humanity, the Herculean intellect not being altogether super-human, nor unlike that of the great contemporary who had to read hard to learn like common mortals.   But whether the gifted being could perceive at a glance what intellectual mediocrity might learn in a lifetime, or not, matters little, for the question is not one depending upon proofs or signs of grammar scholarship, high or low, little Latin, or less Greek, but upon minute mental analysis possible only by rigid comparison of writings.   The dramas are no product of fitful energy or lucky hit, but definite works fairly designed.   In finding *How* and *Why* they were written, the mode and motive proclaim their author.   By him they were wrought as no mere "brain-creation or idle display of power," but "rather to advance the universal work of instauration ;" and they reveal, besides the innate, "labour in inquiry and working" to acquire knowledge.   Though books as guide are by Biròn flouted,

> " Small have continual plodders ever won,
>   Save base authority from other's books,"

they are to Prospero "all his study."   He, like Bacon, is "better able to hold a book than play a part," and "studied books rather than men."   To both books were "brave utensils."   On book lore the three agree.   In 1583–4 Biròn was to

Bacon what in 1622–3 Bacon was to Prospero, a philosophic bookworm full of practical projects. But the former in heydey of youth looks cheerily and hopefully forward ; the latter sadly reflects over where he has failed.   By books, therefore, the poet's mind was well endowed.   Like Bacon, he "had read his leaf."   And, as Ben Jonson's lines aver,

> " A good poet's made as well as born,"

so was his fashioned.   Better than common wonderers, Jonson feels he cannot give Nature more than her due ; art must enjoy a part.

> " For though the poet's matter nature be,
> His art doth give the fashion ; and that he
> Who casts to write a living line, must sweat,—
> Such as thine are,—and strike the second heat
> Upon the Muses' anvil; turn the same,
> And himself with it, that he thinks to frame ;
> Or, for the laurel, he may gain a scorn,—
> For a good poet's made as well as born :
> And such wert thou."

With Horace, Jonson thinks "the true poet must often turn the style," and with Bacon, "alter even when I add."   The hand and mind of an amanuensis go together and leave hardly a blot on transcribing paper to bother a printer or bungling editor.   But such was not the felicity of the mind and hand that laboured, and often re-wrote, to perfite *Hamlet* or *Merry Wives*, from meagre outlines to finished forms ; nor of that other mind and hand that went twelve times together over the new organon, according to the method laid down in Jonson's enigmatic eulogy. Indeed, if that mysteriously-worded panegyric be read between the couplets, it will apply better to Bacon than to any one. To him alone the lines,

> " Triumph, my Britain ! thou hast one to show,
> To whom all scenes of Europe homage owe,"

are appropriate. In 1623 he was the only one in Britain who had Europe's homage, the great, the wise, and the learned flocking in pilgrim-like devotion. When reviled and mocked, defamed and starved by intriguing countrymen, he was adored by the stranger as the intrepid pioneer who did tropically

> " Shake a lance
> As brandish'd at the eyes of ignorance,"

in heroic *Advancement of Learning*, routing an army of grammar scholars watching in the trenches of a decayed scholastic citadel. All the while the fight went on, he in whose borrowed name the words were printed had lain seven years peacefully forgotten in his grave, without an elegy other than the bald auto-epitaph in "pitiful doggerel the sexton might have written." This long and ominous silence was only broken by Jonson's strain commending the great *Folio*. If his verses be not read literally, but be interpreted allusively, as if one person is addressed when another is meant, according to the oblique Ætolian cunning, they aptly fit the reviver of that method in allegoric or dramatic poetry. Either the eulogy by Ben Jonson was thus allusive and not *è facie*,

> " Or, crafty malice might pretend this praise,
>   And think to ruin where it seem'd to raise."

For Bacon, who had small Latin and little Greek compared with ordinary playwriters of the time, is not meted by them. To do him due honour the panegyrist must invoke insolent Greece and haughty Rome, and

> " Call forth thund'ring Æschylus,
>   Euripides, and Sophocles,"

as peers of the poet by whom they were themselves recalled to life again in the re-born drama; for, scant as Bacon's, and the poet's, knowledge of their language may have technically been, it was yet enough to enable both to read them in the original; since, when Greek drama was revived, in essence if not in form, not one of the three great Greek tragic poets had yet been turned into the English tongue.

This occult mode of interpreting Jonson's enigmatic verses leaves them coinciding with Bacon's own exoteric method of veiled meaning, which he was unwilling should become known except to a select few worthy recipients, and also brings them into harmony with what Jonson elsewhere says in his *Discoveries*. For, while his verses declare the drama can bear

> " Comparison
> Of all that insolent Greece or haughty Rome
> Sent forth,"

the *Discoveries* vow that Bacon "is he who hath filled up all numbers, and performed that in our tongue which may be compared or preferred either to insolent Greece or haughty Rome." How then can parity fail between them? Of one, Nature

> " Joyed to wear the dressing of his lines,
> Which were so richly spun;"

the other the Fates had

> " Spun round and full,
> Out of their softest and their whitest wool,"

and both by Jonson are "woven so fit" into one mind and art in the loom of his own loving fancy.

But, although there is a remarkable repetition in Jonson's eulogy and panegyric, there is also an equally observable difference in the more direct descriptions. Of one, everything said in the *Discoveries* is equivocal, baffling all fair editors and common readers, even down to Dyce, who in his latest effort gave up in despair after a futile attempt to explain the blunder,

"Cæsar did never wrong but with just cause;"

but, of the other—"There happened in my time one noble speaker, who was full of gravity in his speaking. His language (where he could spare or pass by a jest) was nobly censorious. No man ever spake more neatly, more pressly, more weightily, or suffered less emptiness, less idleness, in what he uttered. No member of his speech but consisted of his own graces. His hearers could not cough, or look aside from him, without loss. He commanded where he spoke, and had his judges angry and pleased at his devotion. No man had their affections more in his power. The fear of every man that heard him was lest he should make an end."

It would read almost like a paraphrase on these words to repeat after them the description of a character in *King Henry VIII.*, in whom Verulam has already been shown typified :—

> " The gentleman is learn'd, and a most rare speaker ;
> To nature none more bound ; his training such,
> That he may furnish and instruct great teachers,
> And never seek aid out of himself.
> . . . . This man so complete,
> Who was enroll'd 'mongst wonders, and when we,
> Almost with ravish'd listening, could not find
> His hour of speech a minute,"—etc.

It will therefore be observed that, according to Ben Jonson, editor of the first *Folio*, where Bacon could spare or pass by a jest, in an inveterate habit of word-play amid the most serious thoughts or moments, he had the affections so thoroughly under control that he could anger or please at will—a mental trait which forms the grand psychological feature in the drama.

In an appropriating spirit the apocryphal " *Wit Combats* " at the Mermaid Tavern, as merely imagined by Fuller, have been crystallized out of fiction into reality. Like the praises of "Gentle Willy," in Meres's *Tears of the Muses*, that were undoubtedly meant for Philip Sidney, the misapplied encomiums are now of no validity as contemporary testimony in proof of authorship. The same may be said of the rhapsody of words in Barnfield's *Remembrance*, or of the lines by Basse that were wrongly ascribed to Dr. Donne, who was one of Bacon's ardent admirers and finest eulogists. These alleged references by the putative poet's contemporaries are all either pure hearsay, romances, or actual forgeries. One only amongst the whole number conveys external and internal evidence of being perfectly sincere, direct, and genuine; and that is Green's invective on "an upstart crow, beautified with other's feathers." The bitter reproach of a dying man, lying in squalor, and writhing in remorse, must either have been earnest anger or crazy death-bed cursing. But, whatever may have been the state of mind or heart of that terrible imprecator of the "tiger's heart wrapped in a player's hide," there can be no doubt that when Chettle apologized for posthumously printing Green's diatribe on one whom he believed to be a flourishing impostor, and confessed that the angry tirade was "in some displeasure writ," he was only able to adduce a report by "divers of worship," or very respectable persons who testified to an affirmed "facetious grace in writing" in one of whom Chettle himself then personally knew nothing. Not even in Chettle's mean-spirited and unwarrantable retractation is there one confuting word of his quondam comrade's dying asseveration. Profligate as Green undoubtedly was in the glow of health and action, under remorse and disease he may have uttered truth. At any rate, Chettle did not abide by the solemn testament of his friend. Of the informing order of intellect, the craven trader in calumny maligned a dead familiar to propitiate a living customer. The recreant was not content to clear himself from obloquy, but compromised a defenceless memory. If Green had lived a little longer, to print his own pamphlet, no withdrawal of his sarcasm would ever have been made, and then the jay, or peacock, with three strides and a halt, would have been stript of the borrowed plumage that to the dying eye seemed so untruthful and offensive—a seeming none less real even if Green were moved to rancour by a grip of the tiger-heart of the usurer.

Moreover, Green's veracity and perfect sincerity is borne out by a very apparent allusion in *Ratsei's Ghost*, printed anonymously in 1605, to relate how one Ratsey, a notorious highwayman, before being hanged at a country town, tells a strolling player to try his fortune in London, where he would learn to be frugal and thrifty, feed upon all men, but let none feed on him, make his hand stranger to his pocket, his heart slow to perform his tongue's promise; and when he felt his purse well lined, to buy some place of lordship in the country, that, growing weary of playing, his money may then bring him to dignity and reputation, that he need care for no man; no, not for them that before made him proud with speaking their words on the stage. The admonished poor player gives hearty thanks for the knave's advice, in a way to make the colloquy a pointed satire on some well-known worthy who in the way named grew wealthy and became a county magnate. If this satirical passage " plainly allude " to him who went " to London very meanly, and came in time to be exceedingly wealthy," it confirms Green's saying that he made his money by acting, not by writing plays, and by usury.

That he was a sharp usurer is very clear. One borrower writes about buying "some such warys as you may selle presentlye with profet. Yef you bargen with Wm. Sh...... or receve money therfor, brynge your money home that you maye." Another hopes "that our countriman Mr. Wm. Shak. would procure us monei, wc. I will like of, as I shall heare when and wheare and howe; and I prai let not go that occasion, if it mai sorte to ani indifferent condicions. Allso that if monei might be had for 30 or 40l., a lease &c. might be procured. Oh howe can u make doubt of monei, who will not beare xxx. tie or xl. *s.* towardes sutch a match!" It seems the "Loveing countreyman" was "willinge to disburse some monie," and was told "yf we bargaine farther, you shalbe the paie-master yourselfe," and so keep direct control over both the money lent and the security.

Whether the loan at rack rent was got or not is doubtful. The usury laws framed by Bacon had not yet been passed. But since the repeal of those deterring statutes many an admirer of avarice delights to think the idol who lent money and wrote plays for a living was too wary of his means to be captivated by burgher prayer or blandishment that made no " faire marke for him to shoote att, and not unpossible to hitt." Usury and poetry do not oft foregather. Usury is acquisitive and collective; poetry creative and distributive. All the begging letters sent by the wistful townsfolk are fondly kept among the village archives; but none from the money lender are extant as sacred relics. His, if any ever existed, have all vanished. No scrap of that handwriting was ever seen, except perhaps in a signature that amid so much that is spurious may be genuine. He clearly was not of an educating turn. Fair daughter Judith signed not her name, but humbly put "her x mark" to her marriage deed on her wedding day. The poor maid had never

> " Gained
> Of education all the grace "

of a not more lovely Marina. In her case a sordid sire cannot be said to have thought of education as " *the Georgics of the Mind*," in reality or happy metaphor.

In a late searching biography Mr. Dyce rejects much so-called testimony he formerly held genuine. He now repudiates a score or more of alleged facts as "rank forgeries," "more than suspicious documents," "nonsensical stories," and "trash." One notable inventor of "gross forgeries" and "spurious petitions" is exposed as a deliberate offender; and, as already remarked, the once-believed "Wit Combats at the Mermaid Tavern," imagined by Fuller, have no longer any historic worth.

As an honest and able editor, careful in literal citation, Mr. Dyce commands the confidence of every student who cares for candour in a teacher. Yet what is now by him thrown out as worthless or fabulous, though held good or true in his former editions, many others firmly retain. In them "ignorant credulity will not come up to the truth." Nay, it is even fertile in invention. A new book on *Our Old Actors* makes Burbage the original · actor of many a character unheard of till after he was in his grave. Burbage died in 1619, and the characters he is said to have represented were first made known in 1623. The putative creator of those feigned beings retired from London in 1612, and, Mr. Dyce thinks, had then "entirely abandoned dramatic composition." It is quite well known that he became a hard tythe farmer, maltster, and looker after free grazing commons, like any other needy or greedy rother hind.

That an inceptive mind, able to create the drama attributed to it, should abruptly cease operating while in full possession of the faculty, and become idle or wholly inactive in the very prime of life and vigor of health, is no more agreeable to any known law of cerebral function than compatible with experience derived from the entire history of the human mind, and is therefore inconceivable and probably untrue. Guizot calls it a miracle; and so fully is the force of this fatal objection felt that many, with Guizot and Professor Dowden, think their paragon did not let the superb instrument of thought rot in idleness, but allowed brain habit to run on, writing to the end, as high mind tension must do, to the last minute of the allotted three score and ten. Their opinion is, however, gratuitous. The wish is father to the thought. It is opposed to every sifted fact in the later life, and its derogatory avocation. He who started the notion had only "heard" that two plays were written yearly in retirement. But "all occasions do inform against" Ward's fact. For the true theory of ever active mind-work the real poet is his own authority when asking,

> "What is a man,
> If his chief good and market of his time
> Be but to sleep and feed?—a beast, no more.
> Sure, He that made us with such large discourse,
> Looking before and after, gave us not
> That capability and God-like reason
> To fust in us unus'd."

No, no; the goaded mind, driven by its own inherent forces to create grand drama, gains too great momentum in the working to come so suddenly to surcease. The attempt to stop at forty-eight would make every brain and mind chord snap. The sword may wear out its scabbard, but never the temper of the resilient steel. The brilliant intellect that raised the passion storm in *Timon*, and flashed vivid thought into *The Tempest*, sunk not in a night into "beastial oblivion." After the grand climacteric a magician may break his staff, drown his book, and retire with Prospero to his court in a cell or in his Milan, or retreat with Timon to a cave, a philosophic cynic; but if with Bacon an exile ever "can find a world elsewhere," it will be always on the globe intellectual. Never can life's fitful brain-fever have so quick a turn except, as Guizot says, by a miracle. The veteran may lag superfluous on the world's stage, uttering wise saws in weary iteration, or what may not be wisdom with less truth than tongue; but here in neither poetry nor philosophy is any sign of senility or of premature mental decay. On the contrary, the later dramas of the poet, like the later writings of the sage, as Bacon himself affirms, were nerved with vigor, and grew brilliant more and more unto the parting day. In the very year in which the most ærial of all the plays appeared, the prayer was composed that to the finest ear in England read like the sighing of an angel; a *Will* was made in words of real pathos and sublimity, and a beautiful paragraph concerning *Poetry* re-written to exhaust everything that philosophy and good sense could offer on the *Beau Ideal*. Either it was so, or there were double sunsets in one firmament.

But one of those suns would not care to go down in a blaze or burning halo of literary glory. From an early day, biographers say, the glowing luminary longed for no twilight of thought, but only for premature mental eclipse, when he might draw a veil before the noble capability left to fust in him unused, contrary to his own feeling *if* he wrote the fine sentiment spoken by Hamlet ; and thus the paragon of animals yearned to go under Emilia's definition :

> " 'Tis not a year or two shows us a man ;
>   They are all stomachs ; "

or else all one wondrous paradox.

Although the political purpose of the Renascence Drama is clearly enough divined while unfolding the meaning hid beneath the parable in the plays already named, yet others will follow to complete the analytic method of the new commentary. These further instances for the full induction will be taken from among the agreeable and familiar comedies as well as from obscure and recondite tragedies, terrible and sublime, yet all tending to one conclusion, as cumulative proof shall now demonstrate.

XV

TWELFTH NIGHT: OR, WHAT YOU WILL.

" Offences of presumption are the greatest."

" How soon this mightiness meets misery."

" And thus the whirligig of time brings in his revenges."

In illustrating Bacon's definition of dramatic poetry as History made Visible, by the immediate political object of particular plays in the renascence series, an analysis of *Twelfth Night, or, What You Will,* brings clearly out the following criteria :—First, the exact chronology of the comedy ; second, identification of every character ; third, locality of the scene of action ; fourth, special political object aimed at ; fifth, the true authorship.

These several points become evident in detailing every material circumstance connected with the comedy. For example, among the persons represented by false names in allegory are :—

Sir Philip Sidney,	who appears as	Duke Orsino.
Robert Devereux, Earl of Essex	,, ,,	Sebastian.
Sir Francis Knollys	,, ,,	Sir Toby Belch.
Earl of Leicester	,, ,,	Sir Andw. Aguecheek.
Sir Walter Raleigh	,, ,,	Malvolio.
Sir Fulke Greville	,, ,,	Fabian.
Dick Tarleton	,, ,,	Feste, the Clown.
Queen Elizabeth	,, ,,	Olivia.
Penelope Devereux	,, ,,	Viola
Lettice Knollys	,, ,,	Maria.

To identify these leading characters will suffice for the argument without dealing with minor parts ; only adding that the date is 1584, not 1598 ; and the scene London, not Illyria.

The play was printed for the first time in the 1623 *Folio*. As it was never entered at Stationers' Hall, the date of its composition is unknown. Of its performance in public there is no account extant. It never became known to student or actor at an earlier period than the date named. Even now it is accounted a most perplexing play, defying every attempt to make out its locality, costume, or meaning. Yet on every point it is intelligible. The only tradition of its origin comes through a vague entry in a law student's diary about a play having the same title that was once acted at the Middle Temple, but when is uncertain. By a different line of inquiry the date will be found to be the twelfth of December, 1584, or nearly two years before the arrival of the putative author in London. As the comedy was never performed at a public theatre and was never printed, it could not have served any money-making purpose. On the contrary, the fact of its having been privately played as a diversion is suggestive enough that, like other masques and revels from the same pen, it cost the author money and trouble, the usual guerdon of amateur authorship. It therefore quite confutes the stale old mercantile theory of the Renascence Drama, a base and barren notion, sordid and infertile in the brain of commenter, hindering a higher culture and true perception of the aim and origin of these inceptive works. If the play were written for a living by a needy writer, it wholly failed to fulfil that purpose. According to ordinary reckoning the MSS. must have lain by uncared-for over twenty years. By the newer calculation they lay for thirty-eight years unprofitable, and were at length printed through extreme poverty, or stress of actual starvation. To that plight Bacon was, as is already shown, in 1621–2, suddenly brought down. He who had a decade before laid for his King and country the corner-stone of the mightiest monarchy in Europe, and made a new sun to rise in the West, was now himself eclipsed. Hungry and sad, he had to hustle odd old writings to the stationers, whose "fingers itched to be selling," for money to buy a bit of bread. Mind and feeling would now be in a mood greatly altered from the gay and lively spirit that imagined the pretty allegory of the mirthful comedy. If ever Bacon had before indulged in an over-high and sumptuous way of living, the whirligig of time then brought him in something like poetical revenges.

The aim of the dramatist in preparing an agreeable device to entertain a select few at a private reading would naturally be to follow some familiar episode that would be readily apprehended by the auditory, so as to give point to plot and dialogue, and read a lesson in the manners of the time. Without this key the play is "caviare to the general," pleases not the million, and is rarely acted. The leading idea in the comedy is quietly to hint rather than openly inculcate a warning of a sure retribution for unruly conduct, haughty airs, or supercilious manners among those whom Royalty had chosen as favourites. It was a pasquil lampooning the frivolity that derogated from the dignity to be maintained by personal friends of a great Queen and indulgent Sovereign. Their turbulent behaviour contrasted strangely with the refined gaiety Bacon had become familiar with during his three years travelling with the French Court, where he met daily with all who were eminent in learning, art, science or philosophy, and whose worth his own early-ripe genius enabled him to appreciate. From life among a polished people he returned to witness an immense intellectual energy often thrown away in brawling robust rivalry,

> " Fit for the mountains and the barbarous caves,
> Where manners ne'er were preach'd."

These rough ways not only jarred on his own nature, but seemed to him to endanger the reformed institutions whose polity he had lately learned more firmly than ever to defend ; and the safety of the Queen he was taught to revere. That he should contrive an allegory to avert a double peril is in harmony with all his work. The traits are too consummately touched to leave doubt after they are pointed out. That they have been overlooked by inquirers into the meaning of this genial comedy is wonderful; and they will now become so evident to everybody that nobody will doubt having seen them already.

The fatal influence of gallants and adventurers in the national councils to young Francis Bacon soon became apparent. That he saw sedition brewing in many fluttering in the gay throng and foresaw their future treason, is certain; and that he had a painful sense of personal responsibility to the Queen his hortative writings testify. Notable among them was young Walter Raleigh. His fealty not being yet doubted, he had a spur to his zeal in a freak that the Queen had fallen in love with him. Shapely limbs and graceful dancing, ready wit and poetic talent, had already fascinated her; and thinking he had a hint from her for a love-token, the would-be wooer wrote the famous doggerel,

> " Fain would I climb, but that I fear to fall."

To his woeful ballad a tricky maid of honour,

feigning the royal handwriting "much like the character," replied in a rhyming jingle,

> " If thy heart fail thee, do not climb at all."

The affair created great merriment and banter. It is mimicked in Maria's dropped letter in Olivia's garden to gull Malvolio, in whom Raleigh is identified. Young, gay, and dressy, jewelled at every purpoint, he yet seemed a discreet man, though prone to reprove. An uppish manner made him hated. He became a butt for practical jokes, like Malvolio,

> " Upon some stubborn and uncourteous parts "

the courtiers conceived in him. The maids of honour deemed him affected, and thought him a constant time-pleaser, the opposite of genial good-natured Fulke Greville, the Fabian of the comedy. Old Aubrey says of Raleigh that " he was a fine fellow, but his nave was that he was damnable proud," and therefore in that particular his image is here faithfully represented. The challenge from Aguecheek to Sebastian resembles one given in a quarrel fomented at court between two fretful rivals, who gibed each other that "every fool must have his favour," in the form of some pretty ribbon or petty decoration, a source of jealousy as well as of emulation.

Among such a crowd of characters a studiously thoughtful and bookishly sedate looker-on, who " sometimes seeth more than a gamester," would act the part of a true friend by taking the ludicrous view of puerile behaviour in a set of irritable dandies, and, if gifted with dramatic talent, might readily invest the whole surroundings in their comic garb, rather than view them in a serious aspect. That Bacon was largely endowed with rare qualities of the raciest humour, word play, and vivacity such as sparkle throughout the delightful comedy, has already been fully shown, on the very best authority, irrespective altogether of any fresh opinion that may now be offered on his works. That in his best vein the wording of the sham challenge from Aguecheek to Malvolio mocked Raleigh's bombastic style seems to have been all along allowed. The remarkable phrase in it,

" If thou 'thou'st' him some thrice, it will not be amiss,"

hit off his sneering mode of addressing equals.

He "thou'd" them as if they were his inferiors. The trick was turned to vile taunt at his trial, Coke "thou'ing" him to provoke anger; but the despicable artifice that degraded the lawyer before the grandeur of the law utterly failed to ruffle the intended victim's self-controlled temper. But the mean quip is held to have given a hint to the dramatist to insert the words in the dialogue, yet inaccurately; for the comedy having been written long before the trial shows the contrary was the case. The fitting application was clearly discerned by Coke, who quite likely was present at the only performance of the play at the Middle Temple, as he had not long before been called to the bar. The astute artful pleader lacked æsthetic taste to prompt him to dig deeper into the nature of the grand dramatic poem. To the poet the quip was a very "bird bolt" cracked in playful humour; to the hireling for right or wrong, a "cannon ball" fired in deadly precision. That the phrase was in Bacon's vein is undoubted. He says : "It will not be amiss, when the source of any vanity or credulity happens to present itself, to make a note of it." To tempt Malvolio's vanity through his credulity makes Sir Toby tell

Aguecheek to make a note of it as he indites the challenge.

Other phrases tend to the same conclusion. When Sir Toby would hear about Malvolio, Maria called him " sometimes a kind of puritan." And when Sir Andrew answers, "O, if I thought that, I'd beat him like a dog!" Sir Toby asks,— "What, for being a puritan? thy exquisite reason, dear Knight?" But the quarreling Aguecheek, having no exquisite reason, has only "reason good enough." And Maria exclaiming, " The devil a puritan that he is, or anything constant, but a time-pleaser," shows the feeling towards Raleigh entertained by the maids of honour who hated him as women only can hate any coxcomb who thinks all women in love with him, as did the "affectioned ass" in the comedy.

That Maria is no other than the beautiful and clever Lettice Knollys is plain from traits of close resemblance. The sneer at a pragmatic fop strouting hints at what he dare not utter, as in the frump " thought is free" reveals the disdainful puritan. Her pungent simile of one "smiling his face into more lines than are in the new map with the augmentation of the Indies," comparing a new chart showing recent geographical discoveries in America to the sardonic grin of a wily cynic, is quite in Bacon's quaint irony. Raleigh's two pioneer captains returned in September, 1584, from their first exploring voyage; hence the pith of the ready metaphor. The cry "Westward-ho!" is adroit; "Westward-hoe," an old waterman's call for passengers to the West-end, is enlarged to mean emigrants for the new colony westward of the Atlantic. A maid of honour calling aloud "The devil a puritan!" sounds odd to modern ears; but expletives were current counters in polite court talk in those days. Like Maria, Lettice Knollys was a stern puritan, ready to resent a freethinker's jibe at her creed. Atheists, pantheists, and people of all castes of thought were free to speak their minds before a tolerant Queen, who little cared for creeds if she were free of her own. The opinion on puritans put into the mouth of Aguecheek was that of Leicester on the turbulent sect. Far different was Bacon's view. He contemned only "those which we call Brownists, being when they were at the most a very small number of very silly and base people here and there in corners dispersed." Right or wrong, by modern views his cannot be wholly judged. We only compare the play with what he wrote in "*Observations on a Libel.*" To identify the author, not to redargue doctrine, play and state paper are collated. In writing as he did, Bacon very earnestly repelled an attack by the Jesuits on Protestant rule, accusing it of weakness from dissent; while he retaliated that Catholics were more divided into monastic and seminary, priests of superstition and priests of sedition. The fervid state paper of the political philosopher agrees with the polemical dialogue in the political drama. The dramatist makes Aguecheek speak words appropriate to the character represented. They may or may not express his own sentiments. In Aguecheek is then undoubtedly the rather ripe royal lover Leicester, whose peculiarities are sharply delineated, and who, like his double depicted in the play, "had as lief be a Brownist as a Politician."

As surely then as in Maria is well hit off the arch Lettice Knollys, the gay and lovely lady, and "fair maiden" whose beauty was her bane; when in later life rumour said Leicester poisoned her husband, Walter, Earl Essex, to enable him to marry her, so in Aguecheek have we him who did foul play, and in the odd fashion with "Good Mistress Accost" desired better acquaintance. In Maria as Lettice Knollys, and Sir Toby as Sir Francis, we have father and daughter, a relationship not appearing in the play; but the way in which Sir Toby urges Aguecheek to accost Maria is certainly with Sir Francis much in keeping. The near relationship would be disguised in burlesque, and not made too apparent.

That Leicester was the veritable poltroon depicted in Aguecheek is matter of history. When the latter is told to "build his fortunes on the basis of valour," the hint is plainly levelled at Leicester's notorious cowardice, unfitting him for commanding an army, as none knew better than brave Captain Knollys, who had suffered from official blundering, when he was afield; and as was again plainly found true the following year in the campaign in the low countries, when Sidney fell. The two characters Aguecheek and Leicester are of one another typical, with like mannerism they speak each other's words and ways, and they certainly were contemporary.

Of Sir Toby Belch, the character is drawn with equal fidelity from the original, Sir Francis Knollys, a loyal old soldier and stern puritan, ever testy over his creed, as Sir Toby is when Aguecheek mouths at it. The Queen's own cousin by their mother's side, the old *militaire*, by virtue of "consanguinity," took as many and great liberties about the royal household as Sir Toby takes in the domestic arrangements of the Countess Olivia. A brave warrior, who had fought hard aforetime, he was of brusque, blurting, belching, jovial nature, ever ready for practical jocularity, as in setting on a bevy of maids of honour in pranks on pretentious folks, like that turning the plot in the merry lampoon. In good humour he, one night when the maids of honour were unusually obstreperous, walked into their dormitory with his night-cap on, and with a book in his hand paced up and down reading aloud, refusing to retire until the disturbers of his rest promised to go to sleep and be peaceable. He was the very kind of jolly old fellow to join a coquette in playing off a fooling game on a finical coxcomb such as young Raleigh was at the time by all around considered.

Here it may be well to repeat that not by what may now be thought, but only by opinion among contemporaries can the parallel be drawn. In this way alone can History be made visible. There is ever a bias of the mind running beyond the limits of a proposition, and outside logical rule preferring a present to a bygone estimate.

In Duke Orsino can equally be found the "jewel of our court," the valiant Sir Philip Sidney. Both loved to shine in a halo of beauty, art, poetry, and philosophy, music lending a charm to them all. The chivalrous courtier delighted in happy evenings at home, enjoying converse with thoughtful Bruno, and a few kindred souls who formed the famous "*Areiopagus*." He was at the time betrothed to Penelope Devereux, sister to Robert Devereux, the young Earl of Essex. That brother and sister appeared at court together for the first time about 1584, he being then only eighteen, and his sister a little older. Though then the destined bride of Sidney, hard fate and harder friends made Penelope wed another, not to her own affection. May be

<blockquote>
" She never told her love,
But let concealment, like a worm i' the bud,
Feed upon her damask cheek."
</blockquote>

Anyhow, she proved in her early blight how "there is never a pomegranate so fair but conceals a canker-worm in its blossom."

In Viola, Penelope Devereux has an exact life portraiture. What one said of Sidney, the other of Orsino vows:

"Whoe'er I woo, myself would be his wife."

What is said of the pair in the play is similarly told of the pair in the palace. It is a wonderful conjuncture. Penelope and Viola resemble each other in every feature, in a double likeness becoming more telling when set beside the two pictures of Elizabeth and Olivia. By a poetical freedom Olivia is twice styled "fair princess," whose "sovereign thrones" may be "fill'd with one self king;" to whom is brought "no overture of war," and "no taxation of homage," and who might be "crown'd the nonpareil of beauty." That a mere Countess, however adorable, should be designedly or inadvertently addressed as Queen or Princess, might only be poetic liberty of speech allowable in a merry pageant; but it is nevertheless very suggestive of a poet's mind running on the unmarrying maiden queen who is by Viola aptly called

> " The cruell'st she alive,
> If you will lead those graces to the grave,
> And leave the world no copy."

Olivia's near kinsman Sir Toby, and Elizabeth's other near kinsman Sir Francis Knollys, had both heard their kinswoman vow " she'll never match above her degree, neither in estate, years, nor wit;" precisely as did the author of the " *Discourse in praise of the Queen*" declare " a mate of fortune she never took." Sidney preferring Penelope Devereux to Elizabeth, or Orsino taking Viola before Olivia, alike would

> " Let still the woman take
> An elder than herself; so wears she to him,"

in marked allusion to matrimonial projects on the *tapis* between the royal spinster and her juvenile wooers. The proposed Anjou marriage had only a few months before been broken off. Leicester had another love affair on hand. Sidney, Blount, Raleigh, and Essex vied for the venerable coquette, who to the stripplings might have been grand-mother. Therefore, the exclamation,

> " Too old, by heaven ! "

about the " kind of woman" Viola was sentimental

over, was clearly a covert allusion to the disparity of years between Elizabeth and her loving train, and is not of an ill-mated pair autobiographic, as it is by commentators tortured.

Again, when Viola speaks of

> " Beauty truly blent, whose red and white
> Nature's own sweet and cunning hand laid on,"

one cannot help thinking of her in whom prosaic Francis Bacon saw " both roses white and red do as well flourish in her nobility as in her beauty." More delicious flattery Cleopatra herself could not long for. In *Venus and Adonis*, that first heir of the poetical invention, the line

> " More white and red than doves or roses are "

first touched the simile of white and red, according to ordinary reckoning; but it is now doubtful if it did not come out in the praising discourse before it appeared in either poem or comedy. A favourite trop it was with poet and praiser be they one or twain. The poem rings like lines that lift Bacon to the rank of a great poet. That poem was printed in 1593, the year that saw the sudden death of Marlowe, called by Taine the true founder of the dramatic school. All the dramas in his name are not thought his own composing, several bearing the style-mark of the true Renascence Drama. If not written by Marlowe, by whom could they have been written? By Bacon? who only employed Marlowe, as he afterwards taught another, who

> " Learn'd but surety-like, to write for him "

his name in the Stationer's register? In that case, had not Marlowe died, the world would never have heard a word of his successor.

The climax to the wonderful parallel between Elizabeth and Olivia comes when the flattered Countess, or "fair Princess," tells Viola,—

> " O, sir, I will not be so hard-hearted; I will give out divers schedules of my beauty: it shall be inventoried; and every particle and utensil labelled to my will; as, item, two lips indifferent red; item, two grey eyes, with lids to them; item, one neck, one chin, and so forth. Were you sent hither to 'praise me?"

On reading these words is it wonderful to call to mind the items in another inventory? for, be it noted, both Bacon *and* the poet were equally fond of scheduling the personal charms of the fair one upon whom *they* would confer a poet's compliment of favour. Let then the poet's inventory be compared with the following:—

"For the beauty and many graces of her presence, what colours are fine enough for such a portraiture? Let no light poet be used for such a description, but the chastest and the royalest :—

"Of her gait, *Et vera incessu patuit Dea ;*

"Of her voice, *Nec vox hominem sonat ;*

"Of her eye, *Et lætos oculis afflavit honores ;*

"Of her colour, *Indum sanguines veluti violaverit ostro, Si quis ebur ;*

"Of her neck, *Et rosea cervice repulsit;*

"Of her breast, *Veste sinus collecta fluentes ;*

"Of her hair, *Ambrosiæque comæ divinum vertice odorem Spiravere.*

"If this be presumption, let him bear the blame that oweth the verses. What shall I speak of her rare qualities of compliment? which as they be excellent in the things themselves, so they have always besides somewhat of a Queen ; and as Queens use shadows and veils with their rich apparel, methinks in all her qualities there is somewhat that flieth from ostentation, and yet inviteth the mind to contemplate her the more."

Here we have, in an elaborate and glowing picture of a courtly beauty, especial pains taken to show the lady possessor of the charms so very sensitive as to have them well covered with a veil in the presence of a stranger. Therefore, when Viola is at last permitted to approach, Olivia, calling for her gentlewoman says :

"Give me my veil : come throw it o'er my face."

And when Viola prays Olivia,

"Good madam, let me see your face,"

the tantalizing love-touched Olivia replies,

"Have you any commission from your lord to negotiate with my face ? You are now out of your text : but we will draw the curtain, and show you the picture ;"

and, we might add, complete the parallel.

As for the Clown in the play, Sir Toby's comrade in frolic, he clearly is the far-famed comedian and court jester Dick Tarleton, whose career gives a clue to the true nature and exact date of the comedy. When a boy, Dick had been cow-herd on Leicester's father's estate. The Earl's notice was drawn by an attendant to the rustic's native humour, ready wit, and marvellous power of impromptu. Leicester then carried him to London, where he so greatly diverted the Queen that he was at once installed as court jester. Rapidly acquiring vast influence, so he became famous. He could in a while do more to "undumpish" her irate Majesty than all her councillors. He was indeed the incomparable " Feste, the jester, my lord, a fool that the Lady Olivia's father took much delight in." In 1584 he was in full swing as leader of the palace merriment; and when in September of that year the first expedition to Virginia returned, he got some tobacco from one of Raleigh's captains, and in his own comical fashion smoked it as a taking bit of novelty at his own tavern, at the sign of the Saga, Gracious-street, when two customers seeing him reek, and thinking him afire, threw a cup of wine to put it out. A like tale is told of Raleigh's first pipe in England ; but Tarleton's is original. It brought in the custom of smoking tobacco on the stage in the scene where Malvolio rebukes the roisterers. Beyond knowing the thing is always done, none among theatrical people ever can tell why; yet what is to players a mere stage tradition reveals the secret of the drama.

That Tarleton kept a tavern is known ; he combined the trade of vintner along with the office of jester and comedian. Hence local hits are explained. For example, when Viola, like the fair young Penelope Devereux, well fitted for a little girlish gaiety or gentle pleasantry while wearing her male attire, asks the Clown :—

Viola : Save thee, friend, and thy music ! dost thou live by thy tabor ?

Clown : No, sir, I live by the church.

Viola : Art thou a churchman ?

Clown : No such matter, sir ; I do live by the church ; for I do live at my house, and my house doth stand by the church.

At the time of the comedy Tarleton did keep a tavern in Gracechurch-street, or Gracious-street as Stow names it, though it originally was Grass-church-street, from the herb and grass markets held in the yard at the rear of Saint Benet's Church. Whether Tarleton kept the Cross Keys Tavern, the back of which abutted on the wall of All Hallows churchyard, off Lombard-street, or the Saga in Bell Alley, where it would be next door to Saint Denis Backchurch, is uncertain At the other corner from both only a little way off, stands Saint Benet's, or Stone Church, so named because it was the only stone-built church in the neighbourhood, and, by the way, the only church near with a chime of bells, a fact forming another leading link in the chain of evidence identifying the locality; for when the Clown says: " The bells of Saint Bennet, sir, may put you in mind,—one, two, three," so does he put the reader in mind of the place he so plainly describes, a spot far remote from Illyria. Tavern yards were in those days often used as playhouses before regular theatres were built, the first of. which had hardly then been thought of. In the Cross Keys Inn yard Bank's wonderful performing horse *Signior* was bid to pick out the biggest fool in the crowd, and caught Tarleton by the sleeve, when the wit called out, " You are a horse," words for an oddity ever since. Dick Tarleton continued in favour till one day he said, "See, the favourite rules the Sovereign," pointing to Raleigh, who with Leicester was dining with the Queen. The epigram stung so that jesters were forbid the palace. That happened in 1584, and Tarleton never went near the court till his death's day in 1588. In the year 1585, Leicester, Sidney, and Essex went over to the Low Countries where Sidney was killed, dates notable because fixing the chronology of the drama.

Though the scene is ideally Illyria, actual localities are all in London. To a loiterer beguiling time "viewing of the town and the memorials and the things of fame that do renown this city," it is not odd to say,

> "In the south suburb, at the Elephant
> Is best to lodge."

The notion of the *Elephant and Castle* is more suggestive of the famous hostelry than of an imaginary inn of Illyria. The incongruity of a Toby Belch being there is on a par with giving a seaport to Bohemia, as is done in *A Winter's Tale*. But it will be "noted of the finer natures, though lower messes, perchance, are to this business purblind," that the Polixines of that comedy is an allegorical Bohemian, whose country hath neither land nor water, estates nor seaports. The names and places in both comedies, the Illyria of the one and the Bohemia of the other, give merely examples of " using false names in allegory " —Illyrian and Bohemian titles for English places and people in "making a play of court and kingdom," as Bacon explains to have been a common artifice. To argue seriously that the play of *Twelfth Night* is a tale of the Governor of Illyria is arrant nonsense; and to draw any inference therefrom about the poet's ignorance, or that so learned a man as Bacon would not fall into such solecisms as this, or of making Ullyses quote Aristotle, merely shows how flat stolidity will take literally what is meant for metaphor, and blame the author for their own blunder.

Even the title of the comedy has been equally misunderstood, though brimful of meaning. In Professor Dowden's admirable work, from the old standpoint, it is called a mere holiday diversion for a festive season. "And as if to declare more emphatically that it shall be nameless, Shakespeare adds a second title, *Twelfth Night, or, What You Will:* that is (for we need seek no deeper significance)—*Twelfth Night*, or anything you like to call it." This conclusion may suffice for an author who denies these dramas to be in any way susceptible of definition; but it is not agreeable to the explicit words in the play itself, conveying as they clearly do direct reference leading on to a very perfect definition. In singing a snatch from an old song, familiar in London, but unknown in Illyria, "O, the twelfth day of December," Sir Toby denotes one title, and that not Twelfth Night proper, the sixth of January, but only the holiday when the comedy was acted. The second title comes from Olivia, when telling Malvolio to inform importunate Viola, "If it be a suit from the Count, I am sick, or not at home: *What you will*, to dismiss it." This equivocation is quite characteristic of Elizabeth's inveterate habit of putting off every affair, big or trivial, and in procrastinating, of lying and prevaricating without hesitation or compunction. "A falsehood was to her simply an intellectual means of meeting a difficulty." So long as she could defer or hoodwink, or shift from herself risk of a decision, any mignon might with impunity say for her, "*What you will*," a phrase of itself enough to indicate the real meaning of the comedy and bring it within boundary of rigid definition.

It is therefore no surprise at all that Philip of Spain wondered how the policy of England's statesmen, equally with that of the Escurial, could be held in check by "a wanton." The running play on the word "wanton" between Viola and the Clown is also quite remarkable. When he says, "The Lady Olivia has no folly: she will keep no fool, sir, till she be married," the remark is just such another bit of gag as Tarleton would jerk into conversation or set dialogue to entertain a court damsel with. In truth, the more we go into detail the stronger becomes conviction that the play on the private stage at the Middle Temple had form and vitality from the other play going on in real life within the Palace close by. All the characters in the living counterpart of the performance were great at practical waggery, and took "delight at these kickshaws" got up for the Queen's entertainment. At contriving frolicsome pasquils nobody was cleverer or more prolific than the "bashful rather than proud" young lawyer, who had a fertile fund of raciest humour for every occasion.

The young reformer was then busy planning and partly working out his gigantic scheme of bringing philosophy, science, ethics, and politics into harmony with the new faith, remodelling the drama as an auxiliary to his grand enterprise, and a page of the same book.

The allusion by the Clown to the new-fangled doctrine of metempsychosis, then brought into court vogue by Giordano Bruno, as the leading idea in his pantheism, would of itself go far to indicate the author of the dialogue; for in 1583 the renowned Italian was staying in London, a guest of Sir Philip Sidney, and through him a frequent visitor at court. He became a great favourite with the Queen, who often rallied him on his gloomy philosophy. Their free discussions, in which her Majesty delighted and joined with fair dialectic, came off in Bacon's hearing, and his was the ironical wit to turn their Pythagorean dreams into refined histrionic ridicule.

The transmigration of souls conceit had already been hit off in the comedy of *Love's Labour 's Lost* in 1583, to lampoon the eclectic coterie of dreaming psychologists who met at Sidney's house as an Acadame, or Areiopagus, to hear all about Bruno's revelation. Of this they made a fadge, lugging it into every chat until it became of itself a burlesque, an offence that had ceased long before 1598, the ascribed date of the comedy. In 1584 the banter would be appropriate to current topics. Fourteen years later it would be entirely out of season.

Indeed Mr. Dyce shows how the *Love's Labour's Lost* had been acted privately or publicly long before 1598. In this comedy the poet appears to paraphrase many passages from Lily's *Euphues*, turning the fashionable lingo into grotesque nonsense. It is reasonable to think the travestie would be contemporary with the outbreak of an epidemic of diseased talk, rather than fifteen years after the morbid manners died out. The court use of euphuism was in full sway in 1583, a year or two after publication of Lily's book, and was ephemeral, the very ridicule thrown on it by the comedy having helped to cut brief the deformed tongue. Every writer in the literature of the Renascence Drama notes the meaning of Holofornes, and his fine speeches; but hitherto none have by their caricature of *Euphues* dated the comedy.

Ungracious it may appear of Bacon, who may probably have been among them, to caricature the graver pastimes of comrades in speculative philosophy, as well as in courtly life. Yet, if the object were to deter them from going astray into fatal errors in their private lives or public career, as he saw often impending over many whom he tried hard to forewarn of danger, by reflecting in a glass before them on the private stage their ' perilous frivolity, in a clearer mirror of the mind than they might ever otherwise be able to view it, the aim was noble, and in harmony with his new definition of the proper function of reformed drama. The aim was none less laudable though it failed to turn wayward self-willed spirits by counsel or admonition, direct or allegorical. Their "qualities and persons I respect and love, for they are all my particular friends. But now I can only do this duty of a friend to them, to make them know their fault to the full." And well had it been for Sidney, and his ill-fated fair Penelope Devereux, as well as for her brother, for Lettice Knollys, Bruno, and Raleigh, had they hearkened to the tropical admonition from an unknown author.

Of Raleigh, whose downfall is the leading point in the play, Aubrey says, "he was a fine fellow, but his nave was that he was damnable proud." The comedy showed him how "both in divinity and in politics offences of presumption are the greatest," "how soon this mightiness meets misery," and how unerringly "the whirligig of time brings in his revenges," on the then opening-out radical principles of true Baconian ethics, a lesson apt for then and for all time.

Finally, it may be noted that as Malvolio is Steward to the Countess Olivia, so likewise was Raleigh Chamberlain to her prototype Queen Elizabeth ; and both the real personage and his mimic were held worthy functionaries, though equally disliked by their fellows. Oddly enough too, as if there could be no ending of the parallel, both Raleigh and Malvolio are nicknamed "Waters." Thus, when the Clown is disguised as Sir Topas, he tells Malvolio, in the dark cell,—

"Nay, I am for all waters."

The meaning of this expression has never been explained, although it is not far to seek. When Raleigh got superfinely complimented by Spenser, in *Colin Clout*, as the daring " *Shepherd of the Ocean*," and the Queen herself embarked beside him as " *The Lady of the Sea*," she, in drollery for the high-flown flattery, bestowed on her watery comrade the quaint *sobriquet* " *Waters*," in prosaic contrast to the poetical hyperbole of Raleigh's protegé, who doubtless hoped for a little royal favour in return for the new metaphorical title. The Shepherd and Shepherdess of the Ocean made a fine pair personified. It was artful of the poet to employ his muse in the dutiful, if not very dignified, business of his patron ; but the Shepherdess Cynthia shrewdly guessed the motive for coining so many fine phrases in her honour, and rewarded them with a little cold " water " accordingly.

But the charming title " *The Lady of the Sea* " was by no means original, but borrowed from the " *Discourse in Praise of the Queen*," written before the poem *Colin Clout* :—" To make an end where no end is, the shipping of this realm so advanced and made so mighty and potent, as this island is become (as the natural site thereof deserveth) the Lady of the Sea," an appellation again repeated in *Observations on a Libel*.

The command of the sea was a quintessence of universal monarchy, and hence the ruling monarch,—" This and much more hath she merited of her subjects."

The rhyming poet caught the metaphor from the grander and more original poet in prose, applying the fine phrase so coined for him, as borrowers do, in adulation rather than in grateful eulogy. Hence the Queen ridiculed what even to her vanity was fulsome ; and so she naively sprinkled over Raleigh a little of his own favourite poetic element, and so also the merry baptism is repeated in the comedy.

As the main plot of the comedy is a lampoon on Raleigh's inordinate presumption, so is there a subordinate though hardly less prominent device to bring young Essex to the front and promote his candidature for royal attention.   In 1584, when barely eighteen, Essex was brought forward by his stepfather Leicester, to divert the Queen's mind from her overweening favourite, whose greed and meddling became irksome to Ministers, and boded harm to the State.   If a match at marriage had been dreamt of as probable between a lad and a woman who for her years might have been his grandmother, there was, in the all but consummated wedding with the Duke of Anjou, example for it. Whether the Queen ever meant marriage, or only made a politic pretence, to keep hope and adherence ever on the alert, it is certain that at the time every month brought out a new suitor. That a match was prefigured in the incidents in the comedy between Sebastian and Olivia is in harmony with all the points already illustrated; for Sebastian is brother to Viola, as Essex was to Penelope Devereux; and he comes upon the scene fighting for a lady's favour, in a duel wherein Olivia interferes to mar the strife much after the way the Queen took to rebuke Blount and Essex on a like occasion. Then there is the romantic episode of the fatal ring, given in token of affection and as a pledge of future succour in case of imminent danger, as when Olivia says,—

> " Here, wear this jewel for me, 'tis my picture;
> Refuse it not, it hath no tongue to vex you :
> And, I beseech you, come again to-morrow.
> What shall you ask of me that I'll deny,
> That honour, sav'd, may upon asking give ? "

The promise, and the token to make it be redeemed, is exactly the same as that Elizabeth gave to Essex, in love token, with a vow that if ever he forfeited her favour the ring returned would win forgiveness. The tragic end brought about by misadventure when Essex lay condemned in the Tower is not alluded to in the comedy, written ere history was complete. Essex got a ring as did Sebastian, with a promise; and nice points prove one souvenir the other's counterpart. Thus, Olivia says the jewel wears her picture, and adds that

> "It hath no tongue to vex you."

The ring Elizabeth gave likewise wears on its gem an exquisitely beautiful miniature picture of her whose tongue oft did Essex vex. That the jewel had been a true love token is shown by the fatal effect. It cut off the one's head and broke the other's heart. The sentiment was deeper than mere keepsake. If the pair were never wed, neither were Olivia and Sebastian, beyond

> "A contract of eternal bond of love,
> Strengthen'd by interchanging of your rings,"

in betrothal. There was no wedding in play or palace, but in both a bond or contract in ring-plighted troth.

Interpreting the comedy by a projected marriage of Elizabeth and Essex, and also between Sidney and Penelope, as typified by the betrothal in the comedy between Orsino and Viola, the proposed match comes near analogy. For when Olivia bids the Duke, " to think me as well a sister as a wife," the relationship would have been precisely that formed by the double wedding at the court, had they come off; for Olivia says:

> " One day shall crown th' alliance on 's, so please you
> Here at my house, and at my proper cost."

The Duke replying answers :

> " Madam, I am most apt t' embrace your offer ; "

but to Viola he only promises her to be

> " Orsino's mistress and his fancy's queen,"

and the affair came no nearer fulfilment.

Nigh enough akin to real events comes the next occurrence in the comedy, where Fabian freely owns how he and Sir Toby set the trick against Malvolio:

> . " Maria writ
> The letter at *Sir Toby's* great importance
> In recompense whereof he hath married her."

But though Lettice Knollys was a hearty young widow wooed at the time by Leicester, she could not have wed her father, if he were really represented in Sir Toby. Had the text made *Sir Andrew* marry Maria, as he by " good mistress accost" "was adored once too," the verity in play and palace hilarity and weddings would be perfect. The difficulty would easily be got over by a trivial "new reading" not very violently dislocating the text, even possibly restoring one of the many disjointings in the first *Folio*. If Fabian were made to say

" Maria writ
The letter at *Sir Andrew's* great importance,"

the connection would leave the harmony with the context complete. This alteration would be in no way unreasonable, but allowable from the fact that several other speeches of Sir Toby's and Sir Andrew's are wrongly set down, and in like manner need transposing. Besides, to show its propriety, it is Sir Andrew who first moots the challenge and writes the second, Maria offering of her own accord to write the first. Such an alteration would therefore suit the text, and leave it better than as it stands. But we are not now hunting; the reader is up to the proof, and may leap or let the heart faint.

Anyhow, the incidents agree with the *début* of Essex and his sister in 1584; and by thus bringing recognized originals and living likenesses together in play and palace, can be given a particular illustration of the manner in which the poet makes History visible in dramatic allegory.

The analogy also helps to explain why the comedy, like so many other plays in the renascence series, favours the Essex side, rather than Cecil's faction. That Bacon was cynosure of the former is certain. On his pen all looked for the aid he gave so freely, to be covered with ungrateful reproach. At what time friendship between leader and chief began is unknown; but in 1584 they must have known each other. The date of the play, as usually assigned, may appear to forbid the conclusion. But who knows the date? Some reckon it to have been in 1613, from the fact of Sir Toby's saying something about "*an undertaker*" of another's quarrel agreeing with the troubles created by certain political "*undertakers*" about that period. But the reasoning is here as loose as in most other inferences about the dates of plays; for the term "undertaker," in the exact connotation given to it by Sir Toby, occurs in

Bacon's report on the Lopez treason, where the phrase "execrable undertakers" is used to denote braves or assassins hired as mercenaries; so that, as will be further explained when discussing *Hamlet*, before 1590 the term was in political use precisely as in the drama.

Even the flying allusion to "Mrs. Mall's picture" affords full proof neither trite nor trivial of the period of the comedy, and of the inner court-life depicted in it, down to the very by-play. Bantering vain Aguecheek on his flesh-trigged calf and skill in doing "the back trick," kickshaw qualities his prototype Leicester delighted in for having won him more favour than he ever got through statesmanship or valour, Sir Toby twits the mock modesty of the leering wooer by likening it to the valued portrait of some worthy lady carefully screened to keep away the dust. The precise meaning of what is believed to be a direct reference to a notable picture is greatly debated, most critics inclining to think it may have been the likeness of Mrs. Frith, a clever woman who at one time went about London dressed in male attire, and from her calling came to be known by the cognomen of Moll Cutpurse.

But even if a common caricature print hung up in every taproom were ever likely to be covered with a dust-gauze, the picture could hardly have adorned the hostelry of any thrifty vintner earlier than 1601, the epoch of that notorious character. The truer reading will refer the allusion to a portrait of Lady Harrington, wife of Sir John Harrington, the Queen's own godson. This sarcastic wit and clever rhymer, who vexed his godmother by translating *Orlando Furioso* as a *micramos* to amuse her maids of honour, always spoke and wrote of his amiable spouse as " Sweet Mrs. Mall." And comely Mary Rogers was perhaps a little odd among court company for her frugal care of her husband's dogs and poultry, her retiring ways and thrifty disposition. In 1584 nothing in the way of direct simile could be more appropriate than this homely allusion to John and his " Sweet Mall's " carefully-kept picture.

Finally, when the Clown sings to Fabian,

" Hey, Robin, jolly Robin,
Tell me how thy lady does,"

one cannot but think of Sir Fulke Greville, who by freely and good-naturedly taking all blame on himself whenever any waiting-maid "spilt the milk-pail," got called Robin Goodfellow. To connect this nickname with Bacon will need but little trouble. In one of the *Apophthegms* he tells how "Sir Fulke Greville had much and private access to Queen Elizabeth, which he used honourably, and did many men good; yet he would say merrily of himself: *That he was like Robin Goodfellow; for when the maids spilt the milk-pans, or kept any racket, they would lay it upon Robin; so what tales the ladies about the Queen told her, or other bad offices that they did, they would put it upon him.*" The *sobriquet* was taken from that of tricky fairy Puck; but in another *Apophthegm* the same court damsels are said to be likened by Sir Walter Raleigh to "witches: *they could do hurt, but they could do no good.*" In the two apt sayings both Greville and Raleigh appear before ladies of the Privy Chamber and the Bed Chamber of Queen Elizabeth, exactly as Fabian and Malvolio appear before the female characters in the merry pasquil. In play and palace Fabian Greville is beloved, while Malvolio Raleigh is hated for identical good and bad qualities, and both utter words identical with those coined in Bacon's brain.

This is the use Bacon made of apophthegms, these *saltpits* of converse, to sprinkle over discourse for relish. That he had them all in his mind is shown by the marvel of memory in inditing them one afternoon without turning a book. He was a great citer of them in his own talk, and they are sprinkled over every dialogue in the drama.

While the comic part of the plot is new, the serious comes of an Italian novel. How the tale became known to Bacon need be no puzzle, for to him Italian was a second mother tongue, and all its literature familiar.

If, therefore, there be no direct evidence for the theory, there is ample inner proof. Any authentic record, or recovered manuscript, would settle every doubt, without an inference; but discussion from analogy can alone sustain a challenge offered to accredited accounts. The kind of proof agrees with the line of argument taken by Mr. Spedding to determine the authorship of the *Device* ascribed to Essex, of which the *Discourse in Praise of the Queen* is part. If verified inference be fair to one, it must be so to another. To reasoning by sound logic there is not in either case a word repugnant.

Moreover, if the new idea of the play be true—and who can doubt it?—the date forbids the thought of the putative author having had mind or hand in the work. Once, like a play of Æschylos, acted privately at an Inn of Court, and never printed before 1623, it could not until then have ever had a money value. Bought by a stationer, whose trading fingers itched to be selling, it was hurriedly printed, not to keep green the fading memory of a dead actor, but to let live the famished body of a starving genius.

By far-reaching fancy, a youth of nineteen, roistering in a rustic village, might be believed to conjure up before his mental vision every minute detail of town life and courtly intrigue going on among the *élite* of a great capital. But to ascribe that ken to a great poet moving hourly amid action in the "swelling scene," a monarch beheld, needs no effort "an impossible thing to next make plain," it being in itself obvious. On the contrary, to define the political purport of the comedy is to decide the question of authorship.

XVI

HAMLET.

" The woman at the play, touch'd in her conscience, began to cry aloud and shriek, ' Woe is me ! that hits me ; for so it was that I kill'd my innocent husband.' "

" He came too late to this shift, having first bewrayed his guilty conscience in denying deeds proved to his face."

> " The play 's the thing
> Wherein I'll catch the conscience of the King."

I.F the proper part of dramatic allegory be to hold a mirror up to nature, the political playwright will naturally turn his theatre reflector towards the leading good or profligate feature of the time. Hence, for example, when queen-empoisoning *Hamlet* was first heard of, all England was agog hunting or unearthing burrowing assassins hired by the agents of claimants for her Crown to kill the Queen by secret poison. In 1584 three different plots of that regicide sort were detected and blown upon. To preserve the Queen's life and avert the civil war, with overthrow of the reformed religion that would be involved in her death, every loyal subject, whether prelatic or puritan, lived from day to day on the alert, watchful. In the general dread London citizens formed themselves into lawfully-ordered bands to pursue to death any one by whom or for whom attempts were made upon their Queen's life. Loyalty grew fervid as sedition became fanatic. Amid the alarm the devoted friend Francis Bacon wrote to the threatened Queen a letter that links his thoughts to the thoughts of the poet who in the exciting time contrived the appropriate play of *Hamlet*. The epistle runs on saying :—

"Most Gracious Sovereign, and most worthy to be a Sovereign,—Care, one of the natural and true-bred children of unfeigned affection, awaked with these late wicked and barbarous attempts, would needs exercise my pen to your sacred Majesty. . . . The happiness of your present state can be no way encumbered but by your strong factious subjects and your foreign enemies. To suffer them to be strong, with the hope that with reason they will be contented, carries with it but a fair enamelling of a terrible danger."

The poetic author of that warning would readily imagine how "the life of her Majesty God would have in His precious custody;" and the fervid mind, glowing in loyalty and warm with personal affection, could hardly help figuratively vowing,—

> " There's such divinity doth hedge a King,
>   That treason can but peep to what it would."

With like felicity he would readily remodel the taking " points that require more ample handling, like stuff before it be otherwise trimm'd," into the little more rhythmical,—

> " When our deep plots do fail : . . .
>   There's a divinity that shapes our ends,
>   Rough-hew them how we will."

Whether prose and poetry came of one mind cannot be affirmed ; nor yet denied can be the identity in idea and diction. Of external evidence of unity in time and political purpose there is plenty ; in declaring the thoughts and style yield internal evidence, for proof it is enough to appeal to every reader's judgment. The verdict may be given fairly, or played off in frolic, showing, " in the comparisons between Macedon and Monmouth, that the situations, look you, is both alike. If you mark Alexander's life well, Harry of Monmouth's life is come after it indifferent well ; for there is figures in all things ;" and so good-naturedly may punning doubters be left to enjoy their quip, while the fact will abide.

Holding the vaguely-defined, yet onerous post of "ignorant statesman," the volunteer mentor of five-and-twenty entered Parliament, amid hot debates on high treason "upon the Queen's Highness safety." Thus, "the first breath of Bacon's public life was drawn in a very contagious atmosphere of loyalty and anti-popery." In the *magnalia regni* uttered in Hatton's glowing orations, his own poetical temperament would be incited to prepare for the political theatre at an involved university a *Device* to make seditious plotters there harboured "bewray their guilty conscience." In such a play Oxford would feel interest from the fact that two of her graduates—Parsons, the "green-coated Jesuit," and Campian—were prime movers in the regicide conspiracies. Hence it would be appropriate there to reveal by the dramatic mirror the foul inhuman wickedness to be perpetrated by perverted medical art. The learned audience would thoroughly appreciate depicting the wily hypocrite "giving a colour that he was a man that had suffered for his conscience;" and who "stood in state of damnation if he did not perform his vow." Mingled cant and casuistry self-arguing how one would "seldom obtain pardon if one made doubt of the lawfulness or merit of the act, it was enough to cast one headlong down to hell;" one man "kneeling at confession," before another who was eyeing him, and diving into his thoughts; words mumbled about "I pawn my soul for thine;" or of some "desperate wretch and blasphemous exorcist;" with the equivocator's query, "Can the deceiver be deceived?" or, is it right to deceive one who is trying to deceive others?—would be figured before the classical assemblage by the oratory scene where Hamlet says—

> "Now might I do it pat, now he's praying,"

with misgivings in a criminal equivocator self-interrogated,—

> "May one be pardon'd and retain th' offence?"

Ecclesiastical indulgence was the weapon to subvert the new and restore the old faith. Hence, reflecting from the moral mirror, allegory depicts the royal fratricide a devotee of the abjured creed. The orison betrays an obligation in mental reserve, first cardinal doctrine of General Mariana. The second is implied in Hamlet's vow of revenge. The infamous doctrine of bad politic based on false religion impels every fanatic to take a wrong way to right even a royal wrong. Along the *viâ mediâ*, guided by the true science of humanity, came the grand morality of the Renascence Drama. The "sober foresight" of a volunteer statesman looked to the grandeur of a free State in re-moulding public opinion. For him the political stage was a ready forge and intellectual anvil, to fashion the mirror he would hold up to reflect the baleful effect of treason to lawful authority, or ends of mad sedition gained through secret poisoning.

The darkly allusive writing, agreeing with allusions in the drama, now appears so figuratively mysterious that "it is difficult in a world so changed to feel the true importance in relation to the business of that day." It dealt with daily thoughts on "both poisons—as well the spiritual poison of wicked revolution, as the material." That mysterious writing is contained in a letter to "*A Friend living at Padua*," in return for information used in the drama.

In ascribing that letter to Bacon, Mr. Spedding relies on internal evidence "almost as conclusive as would be the discovery of a draft in his own handwriting." The external evidence goes no further than to show that Bacon was in a position to write it. Equally so was he in a position to write the secret poisoning, sedition over-awing drama. The letter refers to the second inquiry held by Bacon into the secret poisoning plots of the time. It narrates the plan followed by Squire, discovered about 1598, a prior inquiry into a like scheme concocted by Parry having been begun fourteen years before.

By comparing these two narratives of secret poisoning attempted on the Queen, with the tragic history of secret poisoning on royalty in the play, is revealed the political object of *Hamlet* as a dramatic allegory making History visible.

At the first blush this may seem a wild proposition, " forcing analogy, and drawing conceited inference." And yet, calmly looked at, it will only " show the relation of the then political parties to the writers for the Elizabethan stage." For example, when " with fears forgetting manners," Hamlet, holding their papers more lawful, would

"unseal their grand commission," the stealthy way
to find out a murderous design of a serviceable
villain, merely figured the cunning that "while
light was still in the clouds, intercepted a little
ticket," that enabled him to "find out royal
knavery." And when Hamlet found himself
"benetted round with villanies," he surely enough
was as one "surrounded with a net-work of
cunning;" the ideas are the same. The loyalty
and learning thus incenting sage and scenic poet
to "devise a new commission," written out fair
"as our statists do," in "a fine Roman hand,"
verily did the State "yeoman's service."

For *Hamlet* he "erected as it were a stage
or theatre" to show the growing crime of secret
murder its own image, and let spectators "join
in pursuit of violent untimely death," making every
citizen unite in helping to "cleanse the land from
blood." Thus were "names and deeds reflected
from the stage, or 'mirror' of the time, and that
by the great showman, or 'mirror'-up-holder of
his age." The play indeed exemplifies the now
admitted truth that in its day "the stage was the
great means for inculcating opinions on all practical
subjects," and that the weapon was so wielded

by the private dramatist. In *Hamlet* the "mirror" was made to reveal the plots and its conspirators to the threatened Queen. It brought them tropically before her eyes, guarding her with prudence, when with "majesty of countenance, mildness, and severity, she suffered them to approach her person, to take a petition of the hand that was conjured for her death."

Therefore, to afford an opportunity for the political dramatist "to show the very age and body of the time his form and pressure" in the most urgent State affair of the moment was the immediate patriotic object of the recondite drama. It conveyed a timely and much-needed warning, by the light of an ever-lit royal "watch-candell," in a dramatic allegory contrived by "a lively imagination guiding a ready pen." Thus were prince, peer, and people duly admonished, and incited to adopt active measures for the personal safety of the Queen, on whose life hung the general security of the State. No readier or better means could be devised for putting all on the alert about perpetrators of a horribly-concocted crime, "undreamt-of in the ancient world, and vilest invention of the new."

That *Hamlet* was hurriedly thrown off in an imperfect form to meet a sudden State exigence is probable for many reasons, amongst which is the great enlargement of the drama after its first appearance. Of it, as of other works, the author could fairly enough declare, " I alter ever when I add." To add and alter was with him a continual habit. The story of the ready hand going with the active mind, without blotting out a line, becomes, by the history of the gradual development known to have occurred in this and other dramas, a demonstrable myth.

The tale of *Hamlet* had long before been extant. That old form the poet adapted to an immediate political object. Neither plot nor character was an entirely new poetical creation, however greatly all were adorned when brought anew, on a special occasion and for a patriotic end, before a select private audience. The university that retained monastic discipline with symbolical theology in the midst of a reformed court and country, and upheld the scholastic authority of Aristotle as firmly as did the Jesuit seminarist, was the fittest place in all England for "erecting as it were a stage or theatre," whereon to perform exemplary *Hamlet*, in a new reading of an old romantic chronicle, adapted as it was addressed to a tenaciously conservative and mediævally scholastic community.

That the play of *Hamlet* as we now have it was first printed in 1603-4 is well enough known; but that a play of the same title had been acted at Oxford in 1585 is matter of inference from allusions to it by a contemporary writer. That primary play, whatever may be traced in its relations to the standard drama, was at all events contemporary with the already cited letter of fealty and alarm for the Queen's personal safety against wicked and barbarous attempts upon her life.

The same or another *Hamlet* was again performed publicly during investigations by a royal commission to which Bacon in the end belonged, then conducting close inquiry, in *The Tower*, into a suspected diabolical attempt to secretly poison Queen Elizabeth, by a band of conspirators headed by Dr. Lopez, the royal or court physician, along with some Portuguese confederates hired by " conveyors " of spy news to the King of Spain. This readily can be shown by simply comparing dates. In 1594 the

Report, written by Bacon, was made; and in 1594 *Hamlet* was performed for the first time in a public theatre, at Newington Butts, as has been found through Henslowe's diary, preserved at Dulwich College, wherein is an entry,—"*9* of June 1594, at hamlet....viii s." That the play here referred to was connected with the present *Hamlet* is believed by capable judges, Knight, Gervinus, Fleahy, and many others.

In 1596 *Hamlet* is satirized in Lodge's *Wit's Miserie*, so that the play must have been ere then on a public or private stage.

In 1594 Bacon entered on a new inquiry about fresh conspiracies to poison the Queen, carried on by a fresh gang who renewed the attempt after Lopez and his confederates were executed. There is no evidence that Bacon was before employed in this service; but he corresponded with Essex on the Lopez inquiry.

On July 20th, 1594, Bacon wrote to the Queen: "In the time I have been made acquainted with this service it hath been my hap to stumble upon somewhat unseen." What was that?

Among papers found at Lambeth are two in his handwriting, docketed by himself. These two documents are all-important testimony in this analogy. They are called " The first fragments of a discourse touching intelligence and the safety of the Queen's person."

In these two fragments Bacon proposed the principal remedies he could think of for extirpating conspiracies. This he would accomplish by " breaking the nest of those fugitive traitors, and filling them full of terror, despair, jealousy, and revolt."

Quickened by solicitude, he adds : " It is time I thought of other remedies which, because in mine own conceit I did not so well allow, I therefore do forbear to express. And so likewise I have thought and thought again of the means to stop and divert as well the attempts of violence as poison. But not knowing how my travel may be accepted, being the unwarranted wishes of a private man, I leave, humbly praying her Majesty's pardon if in the zeal of my simplicity I have roved at things above my aim."

Here is proof of Bacon's anxiety to protect the Queen, by a humane *prevænium*, as he himself phrases all moral prevention, by warning confederates of their danger. Elizabeth was induced by that paper to expostulate against the wicked practice of Spain's Ministers and her own rebels going about to take her life by poisonings and murderings.

To condemn the intercepting of letters as immoral is an easy nineteenth century virtue, seeing there is now no need of it. But the mighty interests that hung upon the Queen's life, the insidious methods employed to take it, with the difficult means of their defeat, made her life, without rigour, never safe for a day. Such are nearly Mr. Spedding's extenuating words. And if Bacon justified intercepting letters to spare both threatened and threatener, so said Hamlet,—

> "My fears forgetting manners, to unseal
> Their grand commission,"

to find, as the cautelous statesman found,—

> "O royal knavery!—an exact command,"—

that a royal head should be struck off, nor stay the grinding of the axe.

Here then are abundant proofs that at the same several dates the same ideas were uppermost in dramatist and silent statesman, both dealing alike with the mysteries of casuistry and secret poisoning of a Queen by a claimant for her Crown. By another line of proof the two may be compared and identified.

In 1587, Nash wrote an "*Epistle to the Gentlemen Students of both Universities*," as a preface to Green's *Menaphon*, in which he refers to "makers of plays and triviall translators," adding, "It is a common practice now-a-days amongst a sort of shifting companions, that runne through every arte and thrive by none, to leave the trade of *Noverint* whereto they were borne, and busie themselves with the endeavours of art, that could scarcelie latinise their necke-verses if they should have neede;" and a little further on an allusion to "whole *Hamlets*," and "handfuls of tragical speeches."

The word *Noverint* is here evidently no satirical nickname, but a direct allusion to some scrivener or lawyer who forsook his calling to try his hand as dramatist; the fact being held to account for the apt legal technicalities in the plays. But, in a book printed in 1587, an allusion to a prior event makes it evident that that event was known some time earlier; so that a play, or a character in a play, called *Hamlet*, was associated with a *Noverint* as its author as early as 1586, or even 1585; and, further, that that author was already well enough known to the satirist, or was at least by him then suspected of being a "triviall translator and shifting companion," creating envy and heartburning amongst the "grammar scholars," Nash, Peel, and Heywood, who clung to monopoly in play-making for trading managers, from whose stock money-earning plays the political drama differed.

Now, "my young lord-keeper" being a born *Noverint*, one of the three great lawyers by descent he himself speaks of, was actually working at the trade whereto he was born when Green's orthodox play tempted Nash to satirize the poaching author of *Hamlet*. A deed of attorney drawn up by his own hand at that date is still extant; and, what is more, it is now known that he actually hawked the document about London, trying to borrow money on mortgage from the money-lenders, who thus came to know him in the city as a *Noverint*. Although he too was a university man, he was yet no graduate, but a lack-Latin who got a degree by favour, the left-out ceremonies provoking sarcastic sallies on him as an amateur outsider competing for histrionic fame with the legitimate dealers in that commodity.

There is therefore quite clear evidence that a remarkable drama entitled *Hamlet*, full of tragical speeches, written by a lawyer who was neither a university graduate nor a regular playwright, but a shifting companion trying his hand at the endeavours of art, was performed at Oxford University in the spring of 1585. There is further the concurring testimony of several of the ablest critics on the literature of the drama that the original draft of the veritable *Hamlet* of all time is to be found in the early adaptation of an old chronicle, a conviction produced by careful study of the organic form found common to both the plays. Therefore it becomes a point worthy of proof that the grand drama was written with the political object of making events in current history visible.

That the inquiry into the methods of conducting secret poisoning by the horde of execrable undertakers hired to assassinate the Queen, and the representative drama are co-related, is evident from the identity of thought running through the plot of the one and the machinations divulged by the other. The " Mouse-trap" was but a trope "tropically" showing how one Gonzago was poisoned by his rival in the garden for his estate, just as one Gonzalo—Gonzalo Gomez—was the real criminal caught in the act of attempting to poison Queen Elizabeth in her palace for her Crown. The inner play is

" The image of a murder done in Vienna."

But Gonzago and Baptista are names peculiar to a land further south, and bear to the real names of the regicides the relation known to lawyers as *idem ·sonans*, an affinity that would be fully understood by a *Noverint*, turned dramatist. This inversion of names of so similar sounds, as from Gonzago the victim, to Gonzalo the secret poisoner, is singularly suggestive of design in a true allegory.

When during the performance of the inner or tropical play the King inquires,—

" Have you heard the argument?
Is there no offence it 't ? "—

he but repeats Queen Elizabeth's query about

another treasonable drama of which Bacon had then to allay her fears. "She had good opinion there was treason in it." In the King in the play and the Queen in the palace there was at work the same mental conflict; and to the "ignorant statesman" alone the Queen's solicitude was known.

In the fencing scene in the play, when the King would drink to Hamlet's better breath,—

"And in the cup an union shall he throw,"—

the foul feint was only a trope figuring the deceit of Dr. Lopez, when treacherously offering the Queen a real "abrazo, which is the compliment of favour," to lay her fear asleep, and "make her secure of him for greater matters," of secret poisoning. In precisely similar a way the King behaves in *Hamlet*, saying :—

"Stay; give me the drink.—Hamlet, this pearl is thine;
Here's to thy health."

"Give him the cup."

But, after sipping himself, he drops in the venene *Abrazo*, or "Union," and then he offers the poisoned chalice to his intended victim. Thus to betray an unsuspecting friend through "the Say-cup of Princes," that ever trusted pledge of good faith, even among newly-reconciled foes, was proffered to both, in each a pretended friendlike token, as it was handed over, being made the medium of conveying deadly secret poison. In the action in the palace and the acting on the stage, subtle poisoning under guise of friendship, and with protestations of great regard, was the leading feature in the royal tragedy. In .the theatrical allegory contemporary palatial History was made visible. The mirror was thus held up before the intriguing Gonzalo to show the criminal his own image, and likewise to let there " be sown an opinion abroad that her Majesty hath much secret intelligence" that the place was "full of spies and false brethren," hatching conspiracies for her assassination by secret poison. Bacon required. "not only good intelligence, but the reputation and fame thereof," to deter from these repeated attempts.

In the whole range of the Renascence Drama, *Hamlet* is the only tragedy dealing with secret poisoning as the only engine of atrocity. In *The Winter's Tale* a royal reprobate drugs a drink to "give his enemy a lasting wink," and by-and-by has a drench of his own poisoned chalice. But it will be shown that the comedy is coupled to the tragedy for the same political object, according to the plan of the series which provides a tragedy and a corelated comedy to bring out every intended aim, on a plan already explained. In *Cymbeline*, the crafty art is also seen at work. And just as *Hamlet* would check Elizabeth's destruction by emissaries sent by her rivals for the crown, so was *A Winter's Tale* able to vindicate her title by showing through a charming allegory, full of homely scenes, the chaste pure life and lawful marriage of her mother; these being the points on which the Queen's title of a true inheritor to the throne of England were being by Spain and Rome, technically, legally, or hypocritically assailed.

If it be true, as is here affirmed, that alike in the play upon the stage, and in the plot within the palace, both artifice and language are the same, it follows that fair proof of the political object aimed at will be found on comparing Bacon's letters and papers with the drama; and that this is true can soon be made evident.

Thus, the pearl that formed the union, abrazo, or mark of favour,

> " Richer than that which four successive kings
>   In Denmark's crown have won,"

was valued at

> "The price in which your pearls are esteemed."

According to Camden, these pearls had been obtained by Dr. Lopez from the King of Spain, to tempt Elizabeth with, and lure her to drink poison mingled with an ordinary beverage used in the customs of courteous salutation. In order to lull her fears about meditated treachery, her trusted physician was bribed to betray his calling, and take advantage of his ready access to the royal presence. In the practice of a doubly-diabolical art this minion of a politician had to offer the gem "with protestations of his fidelity, and which her Majesty, as a princess of magnanimity, not apt to fear or suspicion, returned with gracious words," precisely as does Hamlet, as a Prince of Magnanimity, not open to fear or suspicion, with gracious words decline the jewel cup :—

> " I dare not drink yet, madam; by-and-by."

He would play a bout first; and so he set aside the cup awhile.

Even so again the fate of the Queen in the play, who had not been made aware of the poisoning plot, sets out how "One may sit at table by one for whom poison is prepared, and have a drench of his cup." When fearing no evil, she says:—

"The Queen carouses to thy fortune, Hamlet;"

but instantly the horror-stricken King, observing the fatal error, calls—

"Gertrude, do not drink."

But she, taking no hint, replies—

"I will, my lord; I pray you pardon me."

Then the miscreant, in despair exclaims—

"It is the poison'd cup; it is too late."

Evidently then the Queen in the play is not meant to know anything of the planned secret poisoning, but is in all respects in the very predicament of one who "may sit at table by one for whom poison is prepared, and have a drench of his cup." It is only when poisoned by misadventure in drinking what is prepared for another that she suspects the deadly chalice. With a perfidy that death cannot shock, the smoothly-lying placid hypocrite would have the minions think the Queen had only swooned; but, her maternal solicitude defying his craft, she exclaims :—

> " No, no, the drink, the drink,—O, my dear Hamlet,—
> The drink, the drink !—I am poison'd."

The passive agent of her corrupting partner's villany, the Queen herself is yet innocent of crime. To have made her aware of the poisoning project would have quite destroyed her part in the allegory; for she must be poisoned by mishap in order to illustrate what Bacon so graphically describes, and drink the cup intended for another.

And then again in

> " The treacherous instrument . . .
> Unbated and envenom'd,"

that changed hands in scuffling, was only another form of the "venomous dart that hath both iron and poison."

When Hamlet carelessly inquires

> " These foils have all a length?"

he feels assured all is fair play, until he finds

> " The point envenom'd too !"

Then the horrid truth flits through his thought;
and, glancing for a deadly aim to strike the feigning fencer, calls—

> " Then, venom, to thy work."

The entrapped victim does not now wait to weigh
or ponder over scruples of conscience about
whether or no the culprit be

> " Fit and season'd for his passage ; "

nor yet to bid his weapon know

> " A more horrid hent."

Yet, though he stabs the King, the venom is
more in his own mind than on the weapon of his
vengeance ; as it is with the assassin who has
a poisoned sword for the Queen. At the awful
moment Hamlet's mind is wild with thoughts—

> " Of deaths put on by cunning and forc'd cause,
> And, in the upshot, purposes mistook,
> Fall'n on th' inventors' heads."

He harped on no betraying love, but on

> " This something-settled matter in his heart—
> Upon the talk of the poisoning."

It is hence quite apparent that at every turn
of the drama, whenever it is possible to bring to

the front a dramatic climax and give emphasis to
the political purpose of the allegory, the poet
obtrudes the predominant idea of secret poisoning
as the moral of the tale.

If further proof were needed of the relation
of the play of *Hamlet* to the inquiry set on foot
at the very time when it was written, to detect
and expose the principal and confederates every
year conspiring for the "secret empoisonment of
the Queen," the narratives in the play and the
reports of the results of the inquiry might be yet
more intimately compared to show how they are
all too wonderfully alike to be anything else than
identical.   For example, the King, opening his
foul intent to Laertes, says,—

> " I will work him
> To an exploit, now ripe in my device,
> Under the which he shall not choose but fall :
> And for his death no wind of blame shall breathe ;
> But even his mother shall uncharge the practice,
> And call it accident."

Here the plotting King utters the very quintessence of compliced cunning, and only repeats
particulars found carefully detailed in Bacon's
narratives.   But Laertes suborned, who " will
do 't," would also improve the method, saying

how he would fence in jest and poison in earnest.

> " And for that purpose I'll anoint my sword.
> I bought an unction of a mountebank,
> So mortal, that but dip a knife in it,
> Where it draws blood no cataplasm so rare,
> Collected from all simples that have virtue
> Under the moon, can save the thing from death
> That is but scratch'd withal : I'll touch my point
> With this contagion, that, if I gall him slightly,
> It may be death."

Surely that infamy was " murder under the colour of friendship," as marked as any narrated in Bacon's reports. Hence was Laertes another Squire, who, on opportunity prompting, recollected that he had " taken the remain of some poison with him in a little pot in his portmanteau," ready to lay it near the touch of his victim.

Quickly backing up the wicked ingenuity, the King adds,—

> " I ha't :
> When in your motion you are hot and dry,—
> As make your bouts more violent to that end,—
> And that he calls for drink, I'll have prepar'd him
> A chalice for the nonce; whereon but sipping,
> If he by chance escape your venom'd stuck,
> Our purpose may hold there."

Here have we Bacon's narratives of the cunningly-devised plans, with his convincing commentaries on the motives of secret poisoners aptly illustrated by glowing dramatic allegory. In depicting their plots, he used "fewer words that matter do but drown;" but the few were idiomatic and to the point. Thus, the "base carriers of letters, written in cipher," such as might, if opened, "import no vehement suspicion;" letters "written in jargon or verbal cipher," and in the "interests of an unjust ambition of two mighty potentates," revealed the infamy of the times. Then were "wars, that ought to be prosecuted with honour, stained and infamed with foul and inhuman practice." The councillor's state papers referring to "murder under the colour of friendship,"—the "foulest of felonies,"—"men dying other men's deaths,"—in "foul and cruel murder," were indeed painted with the words and adorned with the thoughts in the play about,—

> "Murder most foul, as in the best it is;
> But this most foul, strange, and unnatural."

And duller should we be than the fat weed that roots itself on Lethe wharf, did we not see it.

When the plaintive Ghost says,—

> "'Tis given out that, sleeping in my orchard,
> A serpent stung me; so the whole ear of Denmark
> Is by a forgèd process of my death
> Rankly abus'd,"

the perturbed spirit only foretells by a few years

how, of another victim murdered by foul and cruel secret poisoning,—" It was given out that Overbury was dead of a foul disease,"—" And so his name poisoned as well as his body."

Thus, when the climax comes, it is brought to point directly to the most hateful of deceits, the perfidy of an " union," or " abrazo " in the poisoned say-cup.   Referring to the deluding " union," the writhing victim, with the bitterest irony in the whole range of tragedy, exclaims—

" Drink off this potion :—is thy union here ? "

To no height more terribly appalling could anger soar; hence, on finding high-pitched resolution beaten by a betraying " union," Hamlet hearkens to Laerte's wailing and moralising over the King's fate, through partaking of " a poison temper'd by himself," with as unerring certainty of effect as any potent reacting ever mingled by Nemesis.   But when the victim commends him to Heaven to make him free of it, he would himself live well in memory, nor be a coward in despair of longer life.   He had achieved one great aim of his life, the discovery of his father's murderer; and but for the treachery of him who now craved forgiveness, he would have lived to

"Revenge his foul and most unnatural murder."

He failed through confiding in an old enemy, who made a false feint of new friendship. Therefore, he would live well in a future fame :—

"Horatio, I am dead;
Thou liv'st; report me and my cause aright
To the unsatisfied."

For, when Horatio would be "more an antique Roman than a Dane," with the "yet some liquor left," he is rebuked by Hamlet :—

"As thou 'rt a man,
Give me the cup; let go; by Heaven, I'll have't.
O good Horatio, what a wounded name,
Things standing thus unknown, shall live behind me!
If thou didst ever hold me in thy heart,
Absent thee from felicity awhile,
And in this harsh world draw thy breath in pain,
To tell my story."

But the story of his blasted life and cruel death is never told aright. For over two centuries his perturbed spirit has been knocking under the floor of men's understanding to hear him tell his own tale; yet in their vain egotism they only stamp and bid the restive soul be "confinéd fast" in peace. They obdurate are, even though, after

"The potent poison quite o'er-crow'd his spirit,"

V

Horatio did this thing "truly deliver."   In the
aptly-pointed epilogue he says :—

> "And let me speak to the yet unknowing world
> How these things came about : so shall you hear
> Of carnal, bloody, and unnatural acts ;
> Of accidental judgments, casual slaughters ;
> Of deaths put on by cunning and forc'd cause ;
> And, in this upshot, purposes mistook
> Fall on th' inventors' heads."

All this would Horatio, as a tried friend and
faithful chronicler, well and "truly deliver ;" and
he would also

> "But let this same be presently perform'd,
> Even while men's minds are wild ; lest more mischance,
> On plots and errors happen."

Here verily is a plain statement of the gist,
motive, or *raison d'etre* of *Hamlet*.   Horatio tells
us the play is to exemplify how

> "Foul deeds will rise,
> Though all the earth o'erwhelm them to men's eyes."

This is the " Deus Vindex " written on the old
drawings of " Babington with his complices,"
inscribed along with the " *Hi mihi sunt comites
quos ipsa pericula ducunt* " —(" These are my
companions, whom their own perils led").

On an old drawing of the time, when the
earliest allusion to *Hamlet* occurs, about 1585,

appear the hanging of one of these conspirators, the disembowelling of another, and five others waiting for death, after the failure of their purpose,

"To cut off one poor Ladie's vital Twine."

A few years later (1592) another drawing shows "Lopaz compounding to poyson the Queen," with the verses—

"But now a private horrid Treason view
  Hatcht by the Pope, the Devil, and a Jew;
  Lopez a Doctor must by Poison do
  What all their Plots have fail'd in hitherto."

In Bacon's long and animated narrative, Lopez is described as having "for a long time professed physic in this land." For "pleasing and pliable behaviour, rather than for any great learning in his faculty, he grew known and favoured in court." Having been court physician long before 1592, he must have been about in 1585, during the Babington and Parry conspiracy; and as a matter of course he would be personally known to Bacon, who was also thereabout every day. Lopez insinuated himself into favour with Don Antonio, and next with the King of Spain, who employed him to administer poison. He became a purveyor of news it imported the Queen's enemies to know. By his nearness and ready access at court he had every facility to learn ; and by the kind confidence of his prey, ready means to betray her.

Evidently, therefore, both Lopez and Bacon were about court during the discovery of the 1585 conspiracy to poison the Queen. That was *Hamlet's* year, and the year of Bacon's letter advising the Queen to guard against secret enemies, conspiring for her death, after the manner of the drama.

Here must now be named an important collateral proof of the relation *Hamlet* had to urgent politics.

In 1594, Bacon, writing again touching the Queen's safety, explicitly urges above all things likely to prevent attempts by hired emissaries from Spain, or English subjects refuged in that dominion, conspiring for her murder, not only good intelligence, but also the reputation and fame thereof. Thus, he writes : " If there be sown an opinion abroad that her Majesty hath much secret intelligence, and that all is full of spies and false brethren, the fugitives will grow into such a mutual jealousy and suspicion one of another as they will not have the confidence to conspire together." With an apology for offering gratuitous counsel, he allows that the " proper counsellors to whom it doth appertain take good care to have due intelligence ; " he yet adds : " Methinks it is not done with that glory and note to the world which was in Mr. Secretary Walsingham's time." Walsingham died in 1590. That master in diplomacy "outbid the Jesuits in their own bow, and over-reached them in their equivocation." In his subtle policy to serve the Queen and defeat every enemy, he spared neither time, trouble, nor expense, maintaining spies and agents in foreign parts, without number. He had an eye and an ear at every key-hole. In 1585 that was his appointed official duty. Like Macbeth, he had a servant fee'd in every house. And, as always happens in organized *espionage*, his own old chamberlain, Poley, was retained by the other side as a domestic spy on his master. Of Polonius, this Poley was the original, as will presently appear

When Earl Leicester went over to the low countries in November, 1585, he took along with him in his grand retinue the company of players that had performed *Hamlet* during the gala week at Oxford in the early part of that year. In the grand reception given to the Earl, among the varied entertainments were poetry, charades, harangues, and allegories incomprehensible. In the following year, 1586, the King of Denmark entertained at Antwerp Cardinal Alphonsus and the Infant of Spain, when *Hamlet* was performed before them. Competent critics allow that the *Hamlet* then acted in English appears to have been translated into German, probably by being written as repeated, and afterwards performed in that language. When the German version is re-translated back into English it presents a near approach to the form printed in 1603, though from certain variations it rather seems to have been originally taken from the manuscript that was common to both, the perfect form of which only is found in the quarto of 1604, the German, and the 1603 London versions being both spurious. When a correct version was given to the world immediately after the appearance of these piratical prints, the motive of the author would be essentially the same as that which under precisely similar circumstances caused Bacon to print *Essays* in

1597, to prevent "the wrong they mought receive by untrue copies." *Hamlet* and *Essays* underwent like evolution after piratical printing.

Hence, in an evident political drift in *Hamlet*, comes the question—Was the play produced in Germany, in 1585, under the title of *Fratricide Punished; or, Prince Hamlet of Denmark*, simultaneously with *Hamlet* in England, in 1585, in each case by the same company of Earl Leicester's players, one of the means referred to by Bacon, of startling conspirators at home and abroad, and awakening them to the light in which their evil deeds were watched in England by the ever vigilant "watch candell"? If *Hamlet* had political relation to attempts to poison the Queen of England in 1585, by hired minions of the King of Spain, equally so would the play have political significance to the hirers of the ruffians, and thus both at home and abroad would news be spread, about warning everybody of the guardian's continual vigilance.

Of another fact literature may now rest certain. The many cunningly-contrived attempts to poison Queen Elizabeth by "execrable undertakers, corrupted by money and conjured by priests ; " "damnable votaries," "with means to perpetrate, and means to conceal" their " Proteus of a disguised and transformed treason," led to the inquiries that enabled the inquirer to become familiar with all their "traitorous gifts."

Hence the marvellous technical accuracy in the play. But that knowledge seems a wonderful possession only to those who can believe it an innate gift of inspiration, divination, or imagination, rather than a vulgar acquirement of a diligent science student. "Over *Hamlet*," says Professor Dowden, the poet "is supposed to have laboured long and carefully." Therefore, adds that genial author, " Don't despise drudgery and dry-as-dust work young poets," as would seem to say the dramatist "who had himself so carefully laboured over his English and Roman histories." And if the imperial intellect that for a patriotic lesson to his country made its political History visible in a rapid panorama had beforehand laboured over that history, how much more needful would it be for him to pudder at anatomy, physiology, and toxicology, to learn to tell the Ghost's story ? Wherever gained, that rare technical knowledge must have been acquired, and could neither have come by reading up in smattered abridgments, nor by chance or hearsay.

In telling the astute method of the secret poisoner, and minutely describing with graphic precision the general symptoms, particular anatomical signs, and invariable *pathogenic* effects of a subtle poison poured into the porches of the ear, the accurate Ghost shows how the secret poisoner came—

> " With juice of cursèd hebenon in a vial,
> And in the porches of mine ear did pour
> The leperous distilment ; whose effect
> Holds such an enmity with blood of man
> That, swift as quicksilver, it courses through
> The natural gates and alleys of the body ;
> And, with a sudden vigour, it doth posset
> And curd, like eager droppings into milk,
> The thin and wholesome blood : so did it mine ;
> And a most instant tetter bark'd about
> Most lazar-like, with vile and loathsome crust,
> All my smooth body."

This graphic account of the toxic action of black henbane is far too accurate to permit belief in its being due merely to an intuitive insight into the toils of nature. Inspiration never taught tangible anatomy ; nor did the divine afflatus ever impart knowledge in exact science. That could only have come by reading, or close observation of the working of the drug by one knowing the intimate anatomy of the human body. No order of genius could ever imagine the pathogenic action of a poison. Doubtless finer intellects are endowed with rare faculties conferring a power of quick study, relieving them from the pain of slower nature. But the story of science is no fairy tale.

It could only be by studying nature or reading books that even a mighty poet learned how atropine and hyoscyamine worked in the human body, no mere imagination, however vivid, ever being able to poetize or realize the manner, although it might prompt the question. In 1585 those deadly alkaloids were unknown, yet they potentially existed in the " leperous distilments " from the old vegetable narcotic " midnight herbs " with which the alexipharmy of the time was very familiar. When poured into the porches of the ear, the toxic effect observed would inform the narrator in the play ; for there was warrant for it when the great original trier, Surgeon Ambrose Paré, got accused of killing King Francis II., the foul young French fellow who through court intrigue got wed to pure-blooded if not pure-thoughted Mary Stuart, and put evil into the girl's head, or else into what ought to have been wiser, because older heads of great people who truly or falsely charged her with dropping the deadly narcotic into the ear of Darnley, the rash on whose dead body having either been caused by that or by small-pox. All this tells how secret political poisoners were expert in the nefarious art, and worked in a precise method ; or, in other words, the allegory in the play is planned on therapeutic principle known only to medical adepts, and is no mere amateur fancy that certainly would blunder, even now after all the benefit got from popular medical lecturing, vainly trying to initiate the common mind into the simplest truths in medicine, which even that encyclopedia the editorial intellect can never fairly apprehend. When the writer once poisoned a cur by dropping nicotine within the porches of the flapping ear, and in a minute made the brute sick and stagger, showing what would happen if a man were " to be used as you use your dog," an incredulous looker on thought the matter belonged to sorcery or magic, so little notion had he of the working of

> " These most poisonous compounds,
> Which are the movers of a languishing death."

But before dealing fully with the knowledge evinced by the poet of the lethal action of drugs and their disease-producing, or *pathogenic* effect, a few words must be premised on the anatomical knowledge required to bring it out. And, truly, the "natural gates and alleys of the body" would be well known to one who likened an "artery to a firm white cord," for that is the true appearance the vessel presents when seen intact; only when laid open is it found to be a tube. Outwardly it looks quite different from a vein. The artery is opaque, the vein diaphanous.

The anatomical truths were learned, not by dissection, but through news of discoveries at Padua, long before Harvey's time. The great perfector of the discovery of the circulation of the blood left Cambridge to study under Fabricius in 1598, twelve years or more after *Hamlet* was written; hence the poet, in dissecting his theme, gained no hint from the English anatomist.

One man in all England held a peculiarly favourable opportunity for obtaining news of the repressed discovery that banished Vesalius, and burnt Servetus. Nicholas Faunt, colleague of Nicholas Bacon, returned from Italy while the

Advancement was preparing. To Faunt, a secretary of Walsingham, the encouncement that drove one daring pioneer anatomist away into exile, and sent another innovator to the stake, would readily offer a point of interest. The discovery had to be quietly mooted among a philosophic few. For so grand a truth in nature amiable theology had no favouring ear. Even Harvey feared he would make all men his enemies for saying the blood ran through the gates and alleys of the body. Science had only begun evolution. The anatomy and physiology of heart, lungs, veins, arteries, and absorbents were only coming out among newest truths in natural theology, to illustrate the doctrine of final causes, by following which, in true induction, they were discovered. He who had just returned from the high seat of physiological learning and undaunted exploration was then "living in London, studying affairs at home, and arranging observations made abroad." He often called on Bacon, then engaged on his earliest philosophical work. The extreme caution required in those severe days, so different from our own happy tolerant times of hearty welcome to new medical truth giving words to thoughts open to theological inference, is shown by reluctant curtailment of many of the finer parts in *The Advancement* to fit the Latin form for entering Italy. Then, as now, forbidding grew of idle fear in evil imagining. A demon lurked in every blood globule, and a heretic bruit was heard in the flapping heart-valve. These innocent organs engendered bad blood; but the science that was hindered by religious controversy was promoted in allegoric drama. By "the strings of the heart" Bacon tried the strength of friendship. In pure and wholesome blood he found no enmity till poisoned by wicked ingenuity. For this came his antidote. To him curdling of blood out of the body would be familiar as to everybody; but the lethal action of poison, like eager droppings into milk, going on within the volume of blood in the vessels, could only be known to a pathologist. The idea lay beyond poetical fancy, without the pale of thought or current of imagination, and wholly within the circle of objective knowledge. The invention of instruments to examine the blood and urine with, as is now done with the microscope and the polariscope, is noted as one of the achievements to be honoured at the museum in the *New Atlantis*.

And equally so is the case with the account of the instant tetter that barked the smooth body with a loathsome crust. The phrase exactly describes the red rash appearing on the skin and fauces in henbane or belladonna poisoning. With the various effects of henbane poisoning the poet is by some thought to have become well acquainted through Dr. Holland's translation of Pliny's *Natural History*, where it is said "an oile is made of the seed thereof, which if it be but dropped into the eares is ynough to trouble the braine." But Holland's work appeared in 1601, and could not have suggested any hint to the writer of the German *Hamlet* of 1585, in which the effect is noted on which the plot turns. If, therefore, the dramatist did take an idea from Pliny, he must have read the original Latin work of that as yet untranslated author, with which Bacon was familiar. It is moreover denied that the drug produces leprous symptoms. This shows that lay and medical men are not always apt amateur toxicologists. Though Pliny does not state so, yet it is true that as a poison henbane acts rapidly, producing a red eruption that runs into little pustules, and black crusts, like plague

spots.   Hence the old belief in its use in plague.
Hence also the quaint whim called homœopathy,
in which Pliny was a believer, and probably first
enouncer of the idea.   The poet defined the
curing conceit in a venerable parable,—

"One fire burns out another's burning."

He also alludes to it in,—

"Take thou a new infection to thine eye,
And the rank poison of the old will die."

But better than all is the fine illustration of moral
by medical truth,—

"And falsehood falsehood cures ; as fire cools fire,
Within the scorchèd veins of one new-burn'd."

Like Bacon, the poet was well read in physic,
and hence his aptitude in quoting its homely
apophthegms and quaint old saws; as well as in
illustrating poetical conceptions by intricate matters
medical, in trivial detail and the grander views
then drawing on a new era in physiological
medicine.   From Pliny both learned the doctrine
of drug antagonism.

Nay, more than even that.   The knowledge
of anatomy and of physiology evinced in the play
was not only minute and accurate, but actually in

advance of the ordinary degree possessed even by leading faculty men of the time. Such a knowledge could only be acquired by one who toiled to " make an anatomy of it, and show the lines and parts which might serve to give a light, though no delight." Along with that familiarity there is also profound skill in toxicology brought in off-hand to adorn the wonderful allegory. The poetical mind had been somehow medically trained to aid imagination in framing the leading incidents in this tragedy. He must have made " a collection of phenomena of surgery, distillations, mineral trials," for a purpose. He wrote familiarly of " chasing men to death by poison after poison, first rose-aker, then arsenic, then mercury sublimate, then sublimate again ; it's a thing would astonish man's nature to hear it. The poets feign the Furies had whips, and that they were corded with poisonous snakes." To scourge to death with snakes " may be truly termed diversity of poisons."

This allusion to the Furies, and their poisonous snakes, resembles the highly ornate and very mythological prologue to the German version of *Hamlet*. In that prelude, dark Night, mother of Evil, bids the Furies stand by her while a King

of the land commits secret murder to possess his
victim's wife and kingdom. They are to be ready
to mingle poison with that foul marriage ; kindle
a fire of revenge ; let the sparks fly over the
whole realm ; entangle kinsmen in the net of crime,
and give joy to hell, so that those who swim in
the sea of murder may soon drown. Then Mægera,
Thisiphone, and Alecto are bid go, begone, hasten,
to fulfil poppy-crowned Queen Hecate's command.

This highly characteristic writing is, in
thought, style, and story, in perfect harmony
with the discourse on *The Wisdom of the
Ancients*, interpreting the political meaning of the
ancient fables. That discourse explains the work
of Nemesis, daughter of Ocean and Night,
precisely as the work is assigned to the goddess
in prologue and drama. And just as the author
of that famous discourse held that those fables
contained a hidden and involved meaning, and
were not composed merely for pleasure, so
beneath his own fable of *Hamlet* there lay a
mystery and an allegory, as is here revealed.

This view becomes all the more certain since
the discovery of buried Mycæna. Relics there
found verify Bacon's idea about a period of high

civilization that had passed away, and been forgotten before the time of Homer. The interpretation was a purely intellectual induction from the nature or final cause of Fable. Bacon knew "well what pliant stuff fable is made of, how freely it will follow any way you please to draw it, and how easily a little dexterity and discourse of wit meanings which it was never meant to bear may be plausibly put upon it."

Even so may it be said of an attempt to give political significance to his own allegory. And yet, exactly as in those. fables, as well in the very frame and· texture of the story as in the propriety of the names by which the persons that figure in it are distinguished, he found a "conformity and connexion with the thing signified;" so do we in *Hamlet* "find a conformity and connexion with the thing signified, as designed and meditated from the first, and purposely shadowed out."

This view the veritably Baconian prologue now makes certain. There indelibly rests the finger-print of the pen that wrote *The Wisdom of the Ancients*. No such prologue accompanies the English version. Why? Would it have given too glaring signs of a common origin with the essay telling how and why the poppy-crowned wife of Morpheus did mingle poison to afflict mankind? Essay and prologue both alike tell how the daughter of Night and Ocean deals with human vicissitudes; and both need only to be read to be identified.

> " Indeed, is 't true?
> Most veritable; therefore look to 't well."

In fine, the poet, like the philosopher, must with Cerimon,—

> " Have studied physic, through which secret art,
>   By turning o'er authorities, he had—
>   Together with his practice—made familiar
>   To him and to his aid the blest infusions
>   That dwell in vegetives, in metals, stones;
>   And he could speak of the disturbances
>   That nature works, and of her cures; which doth give him
>   A more content in course of true delight
>   Than to be thirsty after tottering honour,
>   Or tie his treasure up in silken bags,
>   To please the fool and death."

In both the "mind turneth on other wheels than those of profit;" "despising him who throve by pliable behaviour, rather than by any great learning in his faculty;" or, "who was never suspected of anything worse than writing a foolish prescription;" and both would keenly observe "the aptness of the instrument, or the subtlety and secresy of those that practise with him" the art of the secret professional poisoner, "whereby he might reap the fruit of his wicked treason without evident peril."

"Medicine," not long ago wrote Dr. William Farr, in his own philosophic way, "had great attractions for Bacon, Descartes, Locke, and the great thinkers of the seventeenth century. Its object is to save mankind from the chief evils of life, and to develop the highest faculties of human nature. Nothing stands between it and the truth." Bacon felt himself peculiarly fitted to explore the ways of nature. "My mind has as it were an affinity for natural truth." This he wrote in a diary laying down a systematic course of medical study for himself. And when he added—"Gold put up in heaps was like dung, that when spread over the country fertilized it and produced more wealth," he revealed Cerimon's opinion of the true use of medical knowledge. The kind and amount of that knowledge evinced in Bacon's writings correspond with the kind and amount found everywhere throughout the dramas, an agreement far too fine for any mere coincidence. The poet must have studied physic in the same spirit and degree as the philosopher. In later days, when Bacon framed a law separating apothecaries from grocers, he wrote to a friend,—" You may perhaps think me partial to Potycaries, that have been ever puddering in physic all my life." He and the poet were equally great pudderers in physic too, or else he got his ken of its truths by kind indulgence from the Fairies. When these capricious spinsters span Bacon's intellect out of their finest and their whitest wool, they might have been equally considerate to spare their favourite wit from weary toil to learn Apollo's craft.

As the result either of hard and prolonged study, or of instant inspiration most plenary, there is in *Hamlet* medical lore of the higher order. The Ghost's lecture on anatomy, physiology, pathogeny and therapeutic ; Hamlet's criterion on cross-diagnosis of feigned madness, etiology of alienation, delineation of mental aberration in pure-minded chastity in lewd ravings that,—

> " Strew
> Dangerous conjectures in ill-breeding minds,"

to Hamlet's dishonour, but erroneously held a reason for his antic disposition and affected flight of reason; the desperate appliances needed for diseases desperate grown, the poison of deep grief in the State, in the body, or in mental poisoning, even down to the vulgar crowner's quest, with all its rotten personality, display an acquaintance with matters medical at once accurate and comprehensive.

The news of what went on in Padua, referred to in Bacon's letter to a friend living there, would no doubt include a report of the wonder-stirring discovery by Fabricius, of valves in the veins, acting as flood-gates, to check back-flow of blood. They point to the error of Galen, about a flux and reflux going on in the great vein between the liver and the heart, and eventually led on to the idea of a current running through the vessels of the body. Hence the expression,—

" Courses through
The natural gates and alleys of the body,"

bespeaks a definite idea of a perfect current, as quite distinct from the ancient belief of a tidal flow and ebb, a going and coming to and fro of blood and pneuma, as the earlier medical learning held it, and as it was held in England for more than thirty years after *Hamlet* was written; for it always takes more than a generation of Englishmen to mentally grasp a new fundamental truth in physiology or pathology. Therefore, the very gist of the great physiological truth, finally demonstrated by immortal Harvey, is in the play plainly expressed by the newly-coined idiomated phrase "coursing through," or "circulation," as afterwards translated into a yet more decided Latin derivative. The older notion of the action of the blood is stated in *King John*:—

> " Or if that surly spirit, melancholy,
> Had bak'd thy blood, and made it heavy-thick,
> Which else runs trickling up and down the veins."

To make John speak of gates and alleys would be an anachronism, though *King John* was written ten years later than *Hamlet*. The one play is historical, the other legendary. And though both are used in allegory to make History visible, yet closer adherence to historic fact is required in one than the other. Hence the words of John speak of the older anatomical ideas of his time, while Hamlet is free to discourse on events of the time while the play was being written.

That more was not made of the discovery in philosophical works where the idea is little enlarged upon hardly causes surprise, when it is borne in mind how little the thought struck into the scientific mind of the time. Even forty years later, Harvey, who, at a later period than the date of the play, studied anatomy at Padua, under Fabricius, had to preach, talk about, and show the wonder day by day for over seven years at a London medical school ere he ventured to print, or gained a royal patron's look at the great fact. He was hooted and laughed at as a wild dreamer for bothering his own and other folks' more practical heads with trivial stuff; just as Bacon was twitted by Harvey for "writing philosophy like a Lord Chancellor," in a book of impracticable nonsense that evoked regal bathos about "the peace of God that passeth understanding." So did Bacon rally Gilbert on his universal loadstone; Galileo deny Bacon's theory of tides, because implying an ebb and flow twice a day; and Bacon confute Galileo's, for involving the earth's axial revolution. Such was the chaos of scientific opinion out of which the *Instauration* evolved order. According to Boyle, it was by following the method of discovery indicated by anatomical design that led Harvey, in 1616, to reflect on the function of the valves in the veins, and to enter in his diary a note of what in his mind that structure denoted in respect of use—a note he amplified, and ten years later published. Then Riolan, medical leader of the Sorbonne, bitterly reviled the great naturalist for troubling devout people with his new-fangled atheistical anatomy. Revealed truth, as interpreted by Monks, should be enough for reason. To his dying day Hoffman would never admit a thought of the blood coursing through gates and alleys natural in the body; but steadfastly clung to the orthodox idea of a trickling up and down; and hence, well might thoughtful Bacon fear having written his novel thinking too high over dullards' heads, who did not care to be bothered with elaborating new thought.

To make this part of the argument more complete, it will be well now to revert to a passage in *Coriolanus* not adverted to in the brief note on that play, but purposely left to be dealt with here, in better order, in connection with the knowledge evinced in the drama of the dawning idea of the circulation of the blood; for when Menenius repeats the fable of the belly and the members, as it was either invented by Livy, or narrated by that author from an old legend, and from him copied by Plutarch, the colloquist says of the digested food,—

> " I send it through the rivers of your blood,
>   Even to the court, the heart,—to the seat o' the brain ;
>   And, through the cranks and offices of man,
>   The strongest nerves and small inferior veins
>   From me receive that natural competency
>   Whereby they live."

Now, there is never a word about rivers of blood, heart, brain, nerves, or veins in *Plutarch*, at all events as rendered by Langhorn, Clough, or North, the alleged store-house where the ill-read dramatist is alleged to have gathered second-hand classic lore ; even Livy (then untranslated), who gives the fable, speaks little about " sending to all parts of the body this blood by which we live and possess vigour distributed equally by the veins when perfected by the digestion of the food ;" thus leaving all detail about *rivers of blood*, going to their court the *heart*, then *through cranks* and *small inferior* or *capillary* veins, to be filled in by the physiologist who for other work learned all that was then known about the new idea of the circulating fluid. And it need only be further remarked that Bacon briefly relates the fable, yet in the essay *Of Empire* adding :—" For their merchants, they are *vena porta ;* and if they flourish not, a kingdom may have good limbs, but will have empty veins and nourish little. Taxes and imposts upon them do seldom good to the King's revenue ; for that that he wins in the hundred he leaseth in the shire ; the particular rates being increased, but the total bulk of trading rather decreased." The truth of the Menenian metaphor is, in a medical and literary sense, as entirely lost on Bacon's editors, Ellis and Spedding, as is its grand political meaning and wisdom thrown away on empirics of Parliament, and in tax-brained Victoria abandoned ; but one day rebellion in the belly may carry wiser counsel to ruling heads, and clearer thoughts to literature.

It is no way wonderful, then, that the innovating author of the *Instauration* of learning, who, unlike Riolan, or Hoffmann, was no practical dissector, did not further pursue details in technical biology. But that Bacon held identically the same belief about a current of the blood as did the Ghost and Harvey, is clear from his words in the *History of Life and Death*, written before Harvey's *De Motu Cordis ;* for in that treatise he states that "the blood of the veins supplies the blood of the arteries, and these again the spirit," for oxygen had not yet been heard of, but only vital air.

If Bacon, or the author of *Hamlet*, had desired to demonstrate the blood-flow, either might have contrived some mechanism for the purpose. A toy-like trifle in the form of a hæmoscope could have made the current clear. By a simple experiment of the kind Harvey finally made it plain, as did Lower, a while later, show the cause of the blood in the lungs changing from blue to florid. But, as with many other rapid thoughts in medical theory, verification and adoption long depended upon a capacity for abstract thinking, and ability to weigh evidence. The new inductive philosophy pointed to what experiment eventually verified.

But the author of *Hamlet* evidently knew of the property inhering in the lining membrane of the ear to absorb fluid poison. The writer of the account of the "impoisonment of the pommel of the Queen's saddle, at such time as she should ride abroad," was equally well informed on the absorbing power of the skin; for he says, "In hot July, when the pores and veins were

opened to receive any malign vapour or tincture,"
if her hand touched the part where poison lay,
to bring it in contact with poison laid there for
the purpose. The absorbing function of the skin
in connection with a venous current was a novelty
in physiology, except to a few advanced thinkers
whispering truth to one another within deafened
doors of an academy where new views were
fearfully enounced behind forbidding frowns of a
terrible hierarchy. And though the idea then
dawning on the medical mind of the flow of the
blood might have been picked up casually from
chat by "one that lived in London at ordinaries,
and there learned to argue in table-talk, and so was
very much known in the city," after the gregarious
fashion of a modern literary club, there is yet no
tittle of evidence extant proving that beyond the
Ghost's lips the words had ever been heard of
in England prior to 1585, when *a Hamlet* was
acted at Oxford; and some months later, by the
same players, *a Hamlet*, with the Ghost of a
secretly-poisoned King as leading incident, was
acted at Antwerp.

Of this secret poisoning nothing is said in
the *Historie of Hamlet, Prince of Denmarke*, that

formed the basis for the drama. An English version of the tale appeared in 1570. In it a crafty counsellor aiming at sovereign rule and authority, and respecting neither blood nor amitye, nor caring for virtue, respecting no laws, or majesty divine, secretly assembled conspirators, and slew his brother who sat at a banquet with his friends, and cunningly purged himself of so traitorously detestable a murder to his subjects ; but nothing is said of secret poisoning. That is new in the play.

In the tale no mention is made of veins, or absorbents, or subtile poisons, or coursing of blood through natural gates and alleys of the body ; nor any hint about the work leading on bit by bit, evolving finally the discovery of the circulation of the blood.

There are now no means of knowing the contents of the English *Hamlets* of 1585, 1594, or 1598 ; or whether in them is any reference to the new physiology. But in the German *Hamlet* of 1585-6 the problem is inferentially admitted.

It is equally certain that Bacon dealt with venous absorption as a physiological function forming an integral part of the circulatory system. This he did in his *Report* on the methods of secret poisoning. That elaborate history of the criminal use of poison is a masterly paper on what would now be called *toxicology*, or the science of poisons. Believing the author of that paper to have been simultaneously the author of the empoisoning play, an adequate reason can easily be assigned for his reticence about his relation to the latter work.

The date of *Hamlet* can be determined by the relation of its ethical philosophy to that of Bruno. The two philosophies are identical, as the authors were contemporary. In a grand analysis of Hamlet's finer traits in *Blackwood*, April, 1869, it is affirmed that in real life such an one as Hamlet was Giacomo Leopardi, a mystic traveller between life and' death, impersonating all the doubts and questionings of humanity—a man standing among the wrecks of life so deeply amazed, so confounded and heart-struck, that his trouble paralyzes him, and nothing seems worth doing of all that might be done.

But the poet could not have had in his mind's eye a mystical *doctrinaire* who lived fully two centuries after his own time. The dramatist did not graft Leopardi's spiritual philosophy on his own creation; but if Leopardi's biography, as written by Gladstone, be compared with the life of Giordano Bruno, as given by Saisset, they will be found to be histories of two men of the same mental type and cast of thought, turned adrift by similar vicissitudes of good and bad in fortune. If, therefore, Hamlet be comparable to Leopardi, he must be equally comparable to Bruno, all three being intellectually identical; and if the dramatist had in view a living character from which he drew his ideal of the psychological Dane, Bruno was the man. He was in London in 1585, as has already been mentioned in remarks on *Twelfth Night*. Among other strong peculiarities, Bruno always spoke with marvellous fluency, uttering everything upon his mind; like Hamlet, he held nothing in mental reserve. " His figure was pensive; his traits delicate and fine; a fire-mist of melancholy hung over his brow; he spoke standing; scorning the forms of the school, relying on his fleeing and prompt inspiration, he caught every tone, irony, enthusiasm, sometimes the buffoonery, mixing the sacred with the profane, and coloured metaphysical imagery with poetry." This fitful ethereal being could not have been unlike Hamlet, of whom indeed he formed an admirable prototype. In 1585 Bruno was in the flesh what Hamlet has ever since been in sentiment, a mystic traveller between life and death, carrying doubt and question about humanity to the heart of a people not given to philosophy, "a living example of the serene morality of a virtuous pagan." To Bruno's thinking, there were more things in heaven and earth than are dreamt of in our philosophy, not jeering at it as a flouting atheist, but only as a profoundly philosophic pantheist, ever trusting that natural law will always be equal to its own vindication. Of Monsieur Melancholy, Bruno may well have been the original. Indeed, in his whole career Hamlet agrees in marvellous sympathy with Bruno's feelings and aspirations. In both are found a "brooding being in whose contemplative philosophy and poetry are deep and fine touches of a moody and cheerless, yet noble philosophy—those dazzling flashes of imaginative light which makes all that is around them blaze up with reflected splendour." The opinions of Leopardi given in the *Edinburgh Review*, 1845, and in *Blackwood's Magazine*, 1879, agree; and both are in accord with Falkson and Tschischwitz, that the author of *Hamlet* became acquainted with Bruno's *Candelajo*, in 1583, and other writings, deriving from them material elements on the relativity of evil, and borrowed phrases in Lullian and Brunonian modes of thought.

If, then, there be clearly traceable a close similarity in the philosophy and ways of expressing it, between Hamlet and Bruno, it were easy to understand why Bacon would adapt the dismal pessimism and an optimism full of grandeur to a drama of destiny. Bruno and his colleague Bacon strove together to reform religion, science, and philosophy, or, as some will prefer to say, the logic of the natural sciences, which Bacon held to be true philosophy, there being nothing coming between science and faith ; nor is there. Both were firm opponents of Aristotle, in logic and politic, if not in ethic, denouncing Machiavel, the peripatetic and the Jesuit. On the nature of the soul in man and brute, of the universe, the ultimate efficient, materialism, pantheism, and metaphysic, they were in conflict or perpetual polemic, one abjuring transcending speculations as yielding no exact knowledge, while each had for the other all that was attractive and fascinating ; the common bent of mind appeared more in the view of the sense of right and wrong that forms the basis of true morality, and in the earnestness without melancholy of Telesius, Campanella, and Bruno, with whose joint philosophies the author of *Hamlet* must have been early and late familiar.

In many ways bound by a great mental and moral sympathy, Bacon and Bruno would readily imbibe each other's moods, and repeat their thoughts on fitting opportunity ; as, for example, when early in the spring of 1585 Earl Leicester, as Chancellor of the University of Oxford, gave a royal visitor a grand *fête*, with entertainments appropriate to the character of the University city. Among these were philosophical debates among the Masters. In their exercitations Bruno joined, and, in taking his part, became brilliant in dealing with the question of the immortality and migration of the soul, until the fervor of his eloquence growing unbearable he was abruptly silenced. On quitting Oxford under a ban, Bruno went to Wittenberg, in hope of heartier welcome in the stronghold of the new faith ; and hence the choice of that seat of learning as the *alma mater* of Hamlet and his college comrades.

During this gala season of Oxford, characteristic of Leicester and his times in any affair of regal compliment or festivity, the *Corpus Christi* and All Souls colleges were from day to day the theatre of "*fêtes savantes*," during one of which *a Hamlet* was performed by the Chancellor's players. In August following Earl Leicester went over to the low countries, taking along with him, as usual, the company of players who, as has already been fully explained, acted *Hamlet* in English, their own tongue. Well enough therefore are they poetically said to have taken with them "a whiff of the Shakesperian atmosphere." But, as it unfortunately for the sentiment happens, in 1585 the air of Stratford had not yet parted with the immortal aura; and in carrying on the argument thought yet can breathe in freedom. The logic of dates is inexorable.

With this new idea of the political object of *Hamlet* those dates and biographical records are all-important as crucial tests of the period of the play and true theory of its interpretation; for in 1603 allusions, however indirect, to the peculiar metaphysical views of Bruno would be an eighteen years distant retrospect; while in 1585 they would be aptly pointed. Moreover, with this view and Mr. Plumptre's idea, that *Hamlet* was a covert censure on Mary Stuart, there is nothing incompatible. One rather strengthens the other.

When Campian and Parsons, two Oxford graduates, returned to England on a Jesuitical crusade, getting proselytes among the great nobility, they, as part of their treasonable mission, wrote the atrocious libel on Elizabeth and her government, which Bacon, in masterly " *Observations on a Libel*," effectively confuted. In composing that voluntary and patriotic treatise, the author had to enter into details on the art of secret poisoning, because secret poison was the weapon of the actual tragedy, as it was in allegorical *Hamlet*. It was then, moreover, feared that the Queen of Scots either prompted or connived at the attempts, by emissaries of the King of Spain, to kill her cousin and rival, jealous detainer in hostage, and enemy in religion, by some subtile mode of secret poisoning. Her own husband, Darnley, had fallen a victim to the art. The "black and putrid pustules which broke out all over his body" formed the same tetter that barked most lazar-like with vile and loathsome crust all the smooth body of Hamlet's poisoned father. Quite probably then that rash suggested the thought of showing the effect of secret poisoning by black henbane, in a stage allegory, to deter other like attempts, on the Baconian principle of a sober forethought and wise *prevænium,* making contemporary history for high State purpose visible. The example would be more effective in 1585, while Mary Stuart yet lived, than in 1603, after her trials had long gone among the buried archives of recorded treason. It would also show inferentially that Mary had no more guilty knowledge of Darnley's murder than had Queen Geruth of Hamlet's, both being but passive partakers in wicked results. In dealing with *Macbeth,* it will be found that this was probably Bacon's own opinion.

In 1585, a pandemic wave of secret poisoning swept over European potentates. Of the hour the idea became the favourite fine art. At the diabolical foible, courtiers felt proud to be thought adepts. Thus of Leicester, Parsons declared "He was a rare artist in poison." It was an enviable accomplishment. By seminary priests it was glorified in the eyes of culprits by light from

Paradise in absolution. Guilty or innocent of secret poisonings, rumours of which were hurled as infamies at the royal favourite, the deeds he was accused of, or the fame of them, tell of a prevalent belief in the efficacy of sanctified means to rid the road to a throne by the hand of a zealot who would be "Canónizèd, and worshipp'd as a saint" for the secret murder.

The argument deducible from the similarity of object in drama and state paper can be refined upon by comparing their idioms and diction. This is · the more easily done owing to the highly figurative style in which both are written. Tastes and trifling ornaments reveal traits of character better than plain dealing. Here character is unique. The only duality is in the inevitable changes of form in transition from prose to poetry. In the letter to an English gentleman remaining in Padua, describing the conspiracy of Squire and Walpole, two miscreants who "would mingle heaven and hell," and "lift up the hands of subjects against the anointed of God," Bacon writes,—"This Walpole, carrying a waking and a waiting eye upon those of our nation, to discover and single out fit instruments for the greatest treasons." Even so the wily King in the play astutely avows,—

"Have we, . . .
With one auspicious and one dropping eye,"

pried about to find out fit minions to despatch on a little errand, to do the devil for a royal reprobate. Then is this further added respecting,

"Young Fortinbras,
Holding a weak supposal of our worth,
Or thinking, by our late dear brother's death,
Our state to be disjoint and out of frame."

In the same conceit it is said of the *Libeller* that his end was to round the Pope and the King of Spain in the ear by seeming to tell a tale to the people of England on one hand, and to abuse foreign estates on the other, by making them believe,—

"All is out of joint and ruinous here in England."

The rank duplicity depicted in drama and in state paper was meant to provoke a rebellious rising at home and an invasion from abroad at one and the same moment.

Again, writing on the same engrossing theme, in alluding to providential escapes of the Queen, and to "God's doing and power" in "defending his handmaid and servant," Bacon says,—"He hath done great things by her past ordinary discourse of reason." With this peculiar phrase may be compared the corresponding phrase in the drama,—

"O God! a beast that wants discourse of reason."

In the first quarto, 1603, the words are merely "a beast devoid of reason." This is altered in the 1604 quarto to "discourse of reason," and gives the form that evoked Knight's panegyric, saying,—"The poet must have dropped verse from his mouth as the fairy in the Arabian tales dropped pearls. It appears to have been no effort to him to have changed the whole arrangement of a poetical sentence, and to have inverted its different members; he did this as readily as if he were dealing with prose." This inverting faculty has been shown one of Bacon's prime characteristics. Hence,—"Carrying a waking and a waiting eye," from nervous prose would be readily converted into, "With one auspicious and one dropping eye," in smoothly undulating rhythm.

The other peculiarly fine metaphysical phrase, "discourse of reason," needed no magic touch.

It already lived. Highly prized in drama, it owns in prose the worth accorded to it in poetry. In both it has like connotation. It is relative to human reason. In one, God's providence is seen above "discourse of reason." In the other, animal nature falls below it.

Was the phrase then original to each writer? Or borrowed one from the other? Did not rather prose essayist repeat himself in poetry? It is not in the 1603 quarto: thought a pirated print, as the spoilt phrase tends to prove. The appropriator either could not appreciate the subtle distinction, or lowering the noble metaphysical thought to the level of vulgar apprehension, he purposely brought it down to commonplace "devoid of reason." Long before 1603 the loftier phrase had been employed by Bacon, and it is also found in Tacitus, as rendered by Savill, Bacon's literary intimate, as may be gathered from the letter touching helps to the *Intellectual Powers*, written from one to other about 1596. By Bacon the striking phrase "discourse of reason" was rendered in an English garb before the Latin work had been translated, and ere the edition of *Hamlet* containing it was printed. This, it may perhaps be argued, would afford the putative poet opportunity to glean the phrase from Bacon, and for what it is worth the point may be conceded.

The truth is, *Hamlet* had been acted for the third time in 1598, on a new *fama* of a fresh attempt by Spanish hirelings to get rid of the hated monarch. The meaning of the ambiguous allegory began to dawn on matter-of-fact minds; and gaining a popularity, the text was seized by an adventurous stationer, on the alert for a paying tribute to literature. The garbled version was thus produced as a surreptitious commodity. As with the *Essays*, the author, unwilling to obtrude his works before they were ripe, yet held it best discretion to publish them himself as they passed long ago from his pen, without any further disgrace than came from his own weakness, nor longer " to advēture the wrong they mought receive by untrue copies." On seeing by the vagrant print of 1603 that the work would not stay with its master, he at once played his own Inquisitor, and, in the perfect volume of 1604, gave to literature its grandest study, to humanity its best lesson, and to pagan Nemesis her clearest allegory. The wonderful " profoundly metaphysical phrase " can therefore no longer be extolled as a grand original conception of a mistakenly idolized being.

The following passages offer another example of agreement :—When three leagued rogues "fell in conference touching the empoisoning of the Queen," two of the trio took from the third "a corporal oath, with solemn ceremony, taking his hands between their hands, that he should keep secret that which should be imparted to him, and never reveal the same, though he should be apprehended and questioned."

Even so, when Hamlet takes an oath of Horatio and Marcellus, he bids them,—

> "Come hither, gentlemen,
> And lay your hands again upon my sword :
> Never to speak of this that you have heard,
> Swear by my sword."

Of parallels in legal phraseology little need be said. The skull of the fellow who might have been "in 's time a great buyer of land, with his statutes, his recognizances, his fines, his double vouchers, his recoveries," is thought maybe to have prompted earthy reflections in one grown familiar with legal jargon through his own land conveyances, and that "argal" he was author of the play.

But another land-buyer's poetical attorney did glowingly describe purchases for Sir Thomas Lucy, of Charlcote, fluently dilating on "an abstract of the lands," "lease of great value," "note of tenure," "values, contents, and state, truly and perfectly drawn;" with "scope of acres, woods, rents, and royalties;" winding up by referring to an "assure in jointure;" for, added this pathetic *Noverint*, moralizing while plying the trade whereto *he* was born, "I love not to measure affection to a daughter who might have married to a better living, but never to a better life;" a life Isabella herself might envy, and alluded to in words that Vincentio might borrow:—"Canst thou believe thy living is a life?" in antithesis of his reality.

When about the period of the royal poisoning episodes and earliest private or public performances of *Hamlet*, it happened that Sir Nicholas Bacon was rudely assailed by one of "the traitorous sort," as a man "of crafty wit." In reply, his son, vindicating his father, said the accusation "sheweth that this fellow in his slanders is no good mark-man, but throweth out his words of defiancy without all level;" or, as Hamlet says,—"This fellow hath no feeling of his business." In polity the lord-keeper was "a man, plain, direct, and constant, without all fineness or doubleness;" one who, "in the proceedings of State, would not upon practice circumvent others." In him was very evidently not "a politician one that would circumvent God." The author of *Lear* and *Hamlet* very well knew that the

"Fame and foundation of the English weal"

was never laid down upon the groveling tactic of "a scurvy politician."

In collateral proof that *Hamlet* was written early in the year 1585, a memorable anecdote of that time, alluded to in the play, may be here repeated. "Though it be but a toy"—" a very riband in the cup of" proof, it yet plainly shows the spirit in which the dramatist wrote in his plan of making contemporary History visible in carrying out his grand political design.

In 1585 the feats performed by a wonderful horse were in every eye—"in all the world's new fashion planted." The rare animal was white, and named "Signior," after the fashion of the country it had been brought from. Many very clever tricks made the brute popular, and a good mark for a readily-understood allusion as to a notable occurrence. It would therefore be well enough known what was meant when in the contemporary play the King says,—

> " Two months since,
> " There was a gentleman of Normandy,—
> I've seen myself, and serv'd against the French,
> And they can well on horseback : but this gallant
> Had witchcraft in 't ; he grew unto his seat ;
> And to such wondrous doing brought his horse,
> As he had been incorps'd and demi-natur'd
> With the brave beast."

That the performing horse is here referred to becomes certain from the fact that in the German rendition of *Hamlet*, acted in 1585, the animal is described as "a white Neapolitan horse," and hence its name, " Signior."

Though the animal was still alive in 1601, yet an allusion to its feats performed so far back as 1585 would, late a day, be rather " weary, stale, flat, and unprofitable, among the uses of this world," and as much an anachronism as would be a reference to Tarleton himself, who is by all allowed to be the notorious gagging clown demurred to by Hamlet, while choosing players. In 1585, as will be remembered, that famous comedian had just been thrown out of the post of Court jester, for an infelicitous hit at Leicester, who therefore required for his company of players, in acting *Hamlet*, "those that play your clowns speak no more than is set down for them." In 1585 horse and clown were familiar episodes, fresh in current town-talk, as already fully explained in the notes on *Twelfth Night;* but in 1604 the white Neapolitan horse and his clownish familiar could only linger in the memory as remote retrospects, such as would hardly be effective in a drama making contemporary History visible.

Thus, on every point, so far from being an abstruse poem full of myths, enigmas, and unfathomable philosophy, *Hamlet* is replete with allusions to familiar topics and town commonplaces. Anatomy, physic, law, mythology, and the melancholy mood of a prevailing gloom, were, equally with domestic foibles and effeminate euphuism, redolent of the intellectual atmosphere of the epoch.

Of Osric's euphuistic phrase, it may be added that, if, as is admitted, it be ironical of the fulsome affectation of the time, by Bacon detested, because it was not only in itself absurdly meaningless, but also because it was often associated with insincerity and deceit in arch traitors and fawning courtiers, it would be more appropriately alluded to in 1585, the era of that fantastic speech, than in 1604, many years after the court gibberish had been an obsolete lingo. The same slang is met with in the German play of 1585, although in that country euphuism was practically unknown, a similarity in that particular that proves direct relation between the two works. In the German version Osric is called Fens, and is brother rogue to the. Clown.

In the same form Polonius is called Corambis. The change of name in the 1604 edition, from Corambis to Polonius, is a puzzle to commentators. But it need not be so. The old fribbler played with poison-tipped euphuism, exactly as his pliant son Laertes mal-adroitly fenced with poison-tipped rapier, to gratify the virulent humour of a secret poisoning usurper. In the original drama the name Coram-bis is an apt coinage for a two-faced eavesdropper. That he was privy to the secret ear-poisoning is revealed by the peremptory command to "give o'er the play," in quick words of pricked conscience. For any villainy he was fit, who could make one child a decoy to entrap her lover, and train up another to fence in play and poison in earnest. To Coram-bis "murder under colour of friendship" made the double epithet appropriate. Like Squire, the apt boy, worthy of the father, had "taken the remains of the same poison with him in a little pot ready to lay it near the touch of his victim." Duplicity inhered in the spy-trained Coram-bis family. Stuffed full of high moral precepts, a youth so reared was just the rascal to buy "an unction of a mountebank" to smear the tip of his rapier with to give a mortal scratch as if by accident in playful fencing.

The name Corambis was, like many more in the Renascence Drama, coined in word play to give a verbal definition of the pourtrayed character. Thus were Mal-volio, Ben-volio, formed, as well as Coram-bis. So likewise was the aptest of them all in that way framed; for Des-demona is derived from Greek, and older Sanscrit terms denoting divided affection, the terrible passion in the Asiatic mind, by which the Moor was afflicted, but, as it happily turns out, not at all "for just reasons given," as was Bacon's case when *Othello* was written and Desdemona copied out of an old novel.

It has been averred that if the reason could be found for the change of name from Corambis to

Polonius, by some one familiar with the minor historical characters, subordinate yet effective, of the time, the discovery would enable us to trace the poet home. The alteration to Polonius was made according to the usual mode of employing false names in allegory. It was, as has already been explained, a play upon the real name of one Poley, a chamberlaine in pay of Walsingham, serving the great spy-master as a spy on spies; keeping eye and ear on his employer's keyhole, on behalf of Mary Stuart's 1585 conspirators.

The corresponding thoughts expressed in words, phrases, fragmentary sentences, and even whole passages, here brought into direct comparison, have not been gleaned, picked, gathered, or winnowed from the abundant harvest on the Baconian field; are not selected out of the wide range of voluminous writings varied as the range of human thought; but are every one taken direct from documents of the date of the drama, or pertaining to the matter of which it treats, to which they and it are cognate in import, character, and story, as are "letters written *e re nata*, bearing a synchronism or equality of time," as before said by one of the dual author's severest critics.

There is, therefore, internal and external evidence enough to carry irresistible conviction to any mind washed clear of opinion that the play of *Hamlet* relates to the several inquiries set afoot about 1584-5 to deter secret conspirators from planning an "empoisonment of the Queen." The narratives in play and report are, when compared, found to be not only synchronous, but also alike in purport, spirit, fact, and diction— agreements all too close to be held otherwise than identical. Acting out in epic for a stage or theatre his own defined purpose of dramatic poetry, the author of the graphic anti-queen-poisoning state papers remodels his own mosaic work, and with the recreative touch of the myriad mind, the exquisitely traced golden filligree of anti-prince-poisoning tragedy makes History visible in awe-inspiring allegory, leaving no riddle for Tieck to puzzle over, nor in any way an unfathomable mystery, but plain in clear definition.

XVII

OTHELLO.

"A hook into the nostril of the Ottoman."

"Against the general enemy, Ottoman."

IT was not until late in the year 1621 that the tragedy of *Othello* became known to literature; whether it existed earlier, and, if it did, in what form, are greatly controverted matters; as are likewise the motive of the play, and the true character of its hero. From the days of Rymer, who thought the play barbarous and the hero brutal, till now, when critics, like Guizot, find its taste elegant and the hero noble, albeit a cruel wife-beater, there have been thrown around both play and hero every tint in the halo of literary opinion. Amid the dubiety one cannot be called over-bold to enter another word, nor fearless to rush where angels fear to tread, on a field already trod by every grade of lettered mortal, whose wanderings none need longer follow, but take a new path less errant. The play is said to have been written before 1600, and even acted to entertain Elizabeth in 1602; others declare the date was 1604; while many contend it had no being till 1610; and more, that 1611 or 1614 was the correct era. But all those discrepancies can be got rid of by the magical touch of the mist-clearing word "forgery," a sun that dispels all literary fog. The entries in extracts from accounts of Court revels have recently been proved the grossest forgeries; entries that Staunton, Dyce, and other truthful editors in good faith trustingly admitted with implicit credence; but they were the victims of those literary Iagos who only wrote their works to show how "credulous fools are caught." And much as we may bewail the pity of it, good reader, the sorry truth is there; and now neither a Cunningham entry nor a Collier legend, nor aught save the printed quarto volume can be taken to afford a tittle of evidence to prove the being of this play before 1621, the date of its publication, all entries and inventories having fallen on the inventorers' heads. The poet Jordan made a living by imitating autographs on fly-leaves of relic books, like Florio's *Montaigne*, Bacon's *Essays*, North's *Plutarch;* hence conclude Halliwell and Hallam, "the fabricator of one may have been the ingenious author of others." It is, therefore, truer now than when Steevens wrote about the sixteen plays that "remained unpublished till the *Folio* in the year 1623, though the compiler of a work called *Theatrical Records* mentions different single editions of every one of them before that time. But, as no one else could ever meet with such, I think myself at liberty to suppose the compiler supplied the defects of the list out of his own imagination;" and, therefore, the printer's statement that his original quarto is as the play "hath been diverse times acted" will not unnaturally be looked on as equally gratuitous. There is no mention of *Othello* in Sir Henry Herbert's long list of acted plays, so that if the play did exist earlier than 1621, neither Court nor people made it very popular.

Having, through the candour of editors, made a *tabula rasa* on spurious dates, the reader may inquire what political event arose in 1621 inciting

Bacon to contrive love-sick *Othello*, seemingly void of political bearing. The query can be answered in a word. In June Bacon left the Tower, and got back to Gorhambury, where he had to look out for work that could be quickly done and readily appreciated. Among many literary projects of the time, he had in his mind one dealing with the renewal of events of 1617, and the political troubles daily growing between King and Parliament, to avert an imminent conflict between whom he hoped to engage both along with Spain in a war against the general enemy, Ottoman. In the dialogue on a proposed Holy War, a fragment he might have written any morning, he speaks of the Moors of Valencia as true Christians in all points, save in the thirst for revenge, thus agreeing with the traits drawn in the hero of the play, who is no recanted Mussulman that for love's sake renounced his faith and got Christian baptism. By Bacon the Empire of the Turk is truly affirmed to be barbarous, a cruel tyranny bathed in blood, a heap of vassals and slaves, no nobles, no gentlemen, no freeman, no inheritance of land, no stirp of ancient families, a people that is without natural affection, and that "*regardeth not the desires of woman*," nor "selling her desires" like woman Bianca.

Such are the descriptive words of the writer who pictures the Turks as "a band of Scythian scythes," and invariably alludes to the sensuous nation, without letters, arts, or sciences, with the same feeling as is manifested towards them throughout the drama, instancing them wherever any one's fortunes turn Turk, or make a change for the worse. But although the unnatural affectioned Turk is repeatedly spoken of throughout the drama, it is only in the play of *Othello* where the dyslogistic epithet "Ottomite" is ever employed, and therein it is so applied rather frequently, showing the like fervid hatred of the nation, and ever readiness to

> " Undertake
> These present wars against the Ottomites,"

and rejoicing in every news "importing the mere perdition of the Turkish fleet" to be always animating both the political sage and the equally political dramatist.

The editors of the 1623 *Folio* say *all* the plays had undergone critical ordeal : " These plays have had their trial already," and have " stood out all appeal;" and yet many were till then unheard-of. But it is certain that when Bacon was absolutely starving in poverty the copyright of *Othello* was entered at Stationers' Hall, just before the *Folio* was published. In a short preface to *Othello*, the stationer says he ventured to print the play he would not commend, as the author's name was sufficient to vent the work, which might be left to general censure, exactly in the same apologetic strain as the preface to the *Folio*. Why two patriotic printers should rival each other in yearning to keep green the half-forgotten memory of a dead and gone playwright, and venture unasked to print a posthumous book without hoping for gain, is not so easy to imagine as it is to think of their buying a marketable commodity for their trading fingers that itched to be selling.

The political date and motive of the play will enable any reader to get over many otherwise insuperable difficulties and doubts defying editorial acumen to explain away. Thus the words,—

> " What drugs, what charms,
> What conjurations, and what mighty magic,"

are almost the text of the statute against witch-

craft, enchantment, charm, or sorcery, for gaining
unlawful love, drawn for James by Bacon's own
hand, and repeated when he would codify the
laws; so that there is no need to hint that "the
passage might have been added to the original
copy of the tragedy." The same may be said
of the allusion to the new heraldry,—

> " The hearts of old gave hands :
> But our new heraldry is—hands, not hearts,"

which need neither be looked upon as an interpolation, nor as displacing other words in the
context, putting the date of the play ten years
out of time. Then the lines,—

> " The Anthropophagi, and men whose heads
> Do grow beneath their shoulders,"

are allowed to allude to Raleigh's traveller's
histories, narrated in 1595; but are never
supposed to refer to a revival of their occasion
in 1818, shortly after the traveller returned from
Orinoco. All know the active part Bacon took
in that woeful affair, accusing the returned traveller
of inveracity with disloyalty, and claiming bare
equity in justice for the outraged Spaniard and
his friendly Moor, wantonly beleaguered in the
defenceless homes at Guiana, by English piratical

marauders. In *The Tempest*, written shortly after *Othello*, the same traveller's histories about men whose heads stood on their breasts are spoken of in

"Travellers ne'er did lie,
Though fools at home condemn them;"

and that the allusion is not a personal vindication by the traveller himself, but a taunt by the poet ironically jeering at him, is evident from the context.

In the simile—a trope, by the way, in Bacon *and* the drama far seldomer employed than pure metaphor—in the simile,

"Like to the Pontick sea
Whose icy current and compulsive course
Ne'er keeps retiring ebb, but keeps due on
To the Propontick and the Hellespont,"

editors find an account quoted from Holland's *Pliny*, 1601; but no commenter has observed how keenly Bacon had debated with Galileo the cause of the inflow, in the grand discussion between the two explorers of nature on the cause of the flow and ebb of the tides. To Bacon the icy current inwards through the Gut of Gibraltar was simply matter of familiar knowledge.

One word more on the words "cashiered," "access," and "Sagittary." The first is used by

Bacon early in *The Advancement*, where he glowingly extols Cæsar, resolute with cashiered soldiers, and about the same time by the Host in *Merry Wives*, who associates it with Cæsar, by one or both being taken from the French *casser* to discard. The treatise not being then printed when the play was written, either one writer employed the word in both, or else both adopted it together. Nothing more is heard of the word till employed in *Othello*, after which it became familiar to English readers in South's Divinity writings.

The word "*access*" as met with in *Othello*—"procure me some access"—is used in the way it is employed by Bacon, so often as to bring down on him ill-mannered gibes and ridicule, about 1621 particularly; while the term "*Sagittary*" is so graphic of the archer carved on the archway to the Venice arsenal that critics think the poet looked upon that sculpture; a thing not unlikely, when young Francis Bacon travelled over the continent. True enough,—

> " To vouch this is no proof;
> Without more wider and more overt test,
> Than these thin habits, and poor likelihoods
> Of modern seeming ; "

but they are offered for what they are worth; at all events they are all more agreeable to the life-work and daily thoughts of one who had at heart "the cause of reformed religion, of his native country, of the human race through all their generations; who would be the benefactor of the human race, the propagator of man's empire over the universe, the champion of liberty," as is eloquently claimed for the author of the play, than they are compatible with the daily routine of one who at forty-eight, in the prime of life and health, had only wealthy ease and a few

"Old fond paradoxes, to make fools laugh i' the alehouse."

Although it is well to make the argument complete, yet it cannot be necessary to tell the reader that, the poet having adhered with close imitation to the Italian novel of *Cinthio*, in plot and character, he must have read that author in the original, implying a perfect knowledge of that tongue. It therefore is true enough that "to understand the idea of the poet in the composition of *Othello*, we must disabuse ourselves of some of the common-place principles upon which he has been interpreted;" but the mind must be washed clear of opinion about the authorship, as well as the motive, or political drift.

And now I have done; my literary holiday is over; the recreation may have tired the weary reader with the mind made up; or cheered the fairer reader who may be open to a newer view; both I should gladly have guided a little further, to the next hill-top, to show the valley with Mary of Holyrood and Marina of Mytelene, two fair ones of "chiding nativity," who each could say,—

> " This world to me is like a lasting storm,
>   Whirring me from my friends ; "

whose ill fate hung upon fatal letters in a silver casket; and each "a piece of virtue that would make a puritan of the devil."

Each pretty one of eighteen had rebel nobles, and the inclination of the people, especially the younger sort, each

> " Weav'd the sleided silk
> With fingers long, small, white as milk,
> Or when she would with sharp neel'd wound
> The cambric, which she made more sound
> By hurting it ; or when to the lute
> She sung, and made the night-bird mute,
> That still records with moan ; or when
> She would with rich and constant pen
> Vail to her mistress Dian, still
> This Philoten contends in skill
> With absolute Marina : "

or Mary Stuart as she was on first re-entering Edinburgh at eighteen, after her chase by pirates.

Or we might go on to view the light frail form with "that little hand," the blue-eyed, golden-haired Gruach, the *buidhe* on her native hills or in her own castle, taking a wrong way to right her on feudal wrong, and made therein in allegory a warning to a sister Queen never to "take the shortest way" to right her royal wrong, by imbruing her hand in her kinswoman's blood, while held by her "in double trust."

Tradition tells that *Macbeth*, like the part of the *Oresteia* trilogy it so much resembles, was only acted once before the monarch it was meant to awaken to a sense of fatal danger, and never afterwards was more heard of for over thirty years—1586–1623; fulfilling its end political by not allowing the Queen to "screw her courage to the sticking place;" but making her rather "live a coward in thine own esteem," "letting 'I dare not' wait upon 'I would,' like the poor cat i' the adage." That some unknown deterring influence worked upon Elizabeth is known by her unaccountable behaviour after repeatedly urging Sir Amyas Paulet, Bacon's near relative and ever political monitor, for her sake to "take the shortest way" to rid her of her prisoner-guest and captive rival : her vacillating, relenting, and in remorse punishing the secretary who baulked her purposed mercy. It was not the Queen who pounced upon the caged "Pythoness," but the gloating priest, who mocked at the grey hairs dabbled in blood, as he set the leopard of England on to lap the blood of the Scottish panther. Well might young Francis Bacon, who was privy to all that went on, warn the Queen about the "damned spot" that never would out, and terrify her with an apparition :—

> " Thou canst not say I did it : never shake
> Thy gory locks at me."

The glaring marks of hastive impromptu prove the tragedy to have been hurriedly dashed off in a terrible moment, an effort of a fiery young mind, brilliant with the heat of action amid the scenes it drew. In the bold abrupt style there is no mere stage rhetoric, nor formal eloquence : no speeches precise and vigorous, but feigned and theatrical. The rapid phrase of *Macbeth* flows on like a rugged mountain torrent, leaping from crag to pool, now white with airy foam, now black with solid depth; then held in solemn stillness, till, bounding with melancholy din, it falls, before its course is run, into the loch below and silence.

Contemplating the lonely grandeur of the scene, we shall rest us here awhile, on the Maormor's hill-side, and be thankful.

Naming the plays Renascence drama appeared a pedantry until another writer, applying the fine long Latin word in a book full of folke lore about the English people, gave familiar colour to the novel title. Alluding to the mental force telling on national affairs, and the breadth and largeness which characterize the Renascence, Mr. Green, in his popular History, observes how man then began to know himself, as a human fact, to be an all but infinite power for good or ill; and that the drama towered into sublimity as it painted the strife of mighty forces within the breasts of Othello and Macbeth. Poets passed into metaphysicians as they strove to unravel the workings of conscience within the human soul; and while the sudden popularity of the Bible helped the intellectual development of the people, the disclosure of the stores of Greek literature brought the revolution of the Renascence, as the disclosure of the older mass of Hebrew literature wrought the revolution of the Reformation. Here, then, the word is used in the same connotation as that in which it is employed by me; but Mr. Green omits to add that no writings in that Renascence did more conduce than Bacon's to fill the popular mind of England with these re-born thoughts derived from ancient classics that were before confined to the learned and the favoured few; for those writings of his are a mosaic of classical and Biblical words, gemmed everywhere with patristic quotations, the whole being filled with phrases that have since become ingrained into the mother tongue. And when the plays were planned, it was, as we have seen, "a question whether England should still remain England, or whether it should sink into a vassal of Spain." To avert that fall, the Renascence drama was invented. If Macbeth repealed the Salique law to enable a woman to reign on Scottish or on English land, so was he the first to journey a pilgrim to Rome, and pay his suzeraine an usurper's tribute; hence the political meaning of his bad example for the stirring time when his doings were drawn in allegory; and if the drama bearing his name be full of proud invective, so do Bacon's words glow against deferring to Spain, or doing any act implying England's yielding an obeisance to the trampling monarch.

And even as with the historian, so with the biographer; for the reader of Spedding's life cannot fail to note how oft that editor brings his author *and* the poet into harmony—an accord worthy of one more instance ere we have done. In the *History of King Henry VII.*, to the passage—" Nay, himself, with long and continual counterfeiting and with often telling a lie, was turned, by habit, almost into the thing he seemed to be, and from a liar to a believer, that he was indeed the Duke,"—the editor adds that the poet in *The Tempest* has the same thought—

" Like one
Who having unto Truth, by telling oft,
Made such a sinner of his memory,
To credit his own lie, he did believe
He was indeed the Duke."

It has already been shown that that History and the Drama were written all in a year!

It need only be further noted that every quarto was originally printed as it had been composed, in the form of an epic poem, and never as an acting play, each work being afterwards divided into acts and scenes by practical players, whose adaptations for the theatre were again often altered to suit vulgar liking, by inferior playwrights, who threw the grand poems into sorry travesties that still retain their hold within the playhouse till this day; all things showing the author was no mere actor fitting verse to stage carpentry for a living; but an epic poet knowing about exits and entrances only as might be looked for in an amateur.

With the poet's aim made clear, his lesson is plain, and a people once learning and ever remembering it never can lose the spirit of true freedom. The press may boast of the liberty it conserves while it is allowed to remain free; but it will not forget how stage and pulpit helped, alike by allegory, to win it freedom : will recollect when "the licensed press was closed to the proceedings and preachings of conventicles;" and will remember who warmly remonstrated, at peril of personal safety, with an unwilling monarch to let the preacher go about unhindered by a bishop, to preach the very liberty the press now boasts of enjoying. The free press is the first engine the tyrant turns against freedom of speech, because it is corruptive and buyable when a mere bit of mercantile machinery. Against sedition and shackles the ethic of her drama is England's safeguard; by obeying it she will order the world, and in that way be to herself true. If the behest be denied or ignored by act akin in effect, if not in fact, to another revoked edict; or if evil counsel let atheism and superstition again pair to breed internecion and rebellion, another tragedy played upon the world's wide stage will remind the actors how and why the plays were written.

FINIS.